# The Malthouses of Ware

Also by David Perman

*A New History of Ware:
its people and its buildings* (2010)

*600 Years of Charity:
a brief history of the Ware Charity Trustees* (1991)

with Stephen Jeffery-Poulter
*Ware Through Time* (2012)

# The Malthouses of Ware

## David Perman

Rockingham Press
*in association with*
Ware Museum

Published in 2017 by
Rockingham Press
11 Musley Lane,
Ware, Herts SG12 7EN

British Library Cataloguing-in-Publication Data

A catalogue record for this book
is available from the British Library

**ISBN  978-1-904851-68-4**

Title page illustration:

*The Southern Malting at Kibes Lane*
by Ron Kenway

# Contents

*A forest of malting cowls as seen from the Ware Workhouse – later Western House, now the Octagon – in about 1900.*

# Introduction: a Malting Landscape

The words 'malting', 'malthouse' and 'kiln' are liberally scattered throughout Ware. They occur on buildings of many different types, including a surgery and even a pub. In most cases – though not all – the name indicates that the building was formerly used for making that strange substance known as malt. Consequently the owner or other persons using the building may wonder what the building was like in its former existence. They may also ask more basic questions: 'what is malt? how was malt made? who were the customers for the malt?'

What they may not appreciate is that at one time the whole town was a malting landscape. If you looked down on Ware from any of the surrounding hills you would see a forest of kiln cowls – like the view in the photograph above. Every possible plot of land was pressed into service for a malthouse and kiln. In 1880 there were more than a hundred malt kilns in the town. Throughout the winter the sweet smells of barley and malt hung over everything. Almost every inhabitant was somehow engaged in the industry – working in malt-making, financing it, supplying building materials like bricks and wire floors, providing horses and carts, operating or loading the barges that took the malt to

London or just running one of the many small ale houses which opened at 5 a.m. for maltmakers going to light the kiln fires – working in the hot, dry malthouses was thirsty work.

This book is not a comprehensive history of the Ware malting industry – that has still to be written. It is intended to give an impression of the town in the great days of its malting history. After all, every three-hundred-and-seventieth British soldier or sailor fighting in the American War of Independence was paid for by Ware maltsters through the Malt Tax. It is also intended to answer some of the questions visitors to Ware Museum may ask about the industry. In that task, I wish to record my thanks to Beryl Gafney, Josie Fish, Lis Barratt and Diana Perkins. I have also been helped considerably by the records of the late Jerome Murphy, chief chemist for Henry Page & Co., which were lent to me by his widow, Nan Murphy. I would also like to record my thanks to the staff of Hertfordshire Archives and Local Studies (HALS) and of the Suffolk Record Office at Ipwich, both of which hold the records of many Ware maltsters. I also thank English Heritage for allowing me to use the aerial photograph on page 86, and Andy Gammon for the cut-away drawing of the Southern Malting on page 87.

# What is Malt?

Malt is one of our basic foodstuffs. It is the main ingredient for brewing beer and distilling whisky, but it is also used in other foods such as cereals and biscuits. Malt is partially germinated grain, usually barley, halted from germinating further by being dried with hot air over a kiln. During germination starch cells in the grain are broken down to produce a sugar called 'maltose' which is fermented with yeast in brewing. Malt produces the alcohol in beer but also gives it the flavour and colour.

# Floor malting

The traditional method of making malt was in a 'floor malting'. Most of the malthouses in Ware were floor maltings. Before starting to malt, the barley was cleaned of any grit or broken corns by passing it through a screening machine (see page 11). It was then 'steeped' in a cistern of water for about 56 hours – at the end of which the grain was approximately 45% moisture. The cistern was then drained and the grain thrown on to the working floors of the malthouse for the 'flooring' stage – usually half of the batch on to the ground floor and the other half on the floor above.

In the first stage the grain was piled deep in order to generate heat and stimulate chitting or sprouting. Before 1880 while the Malt Tax was in force, this stage was known as 'couching'. By the end of the couching period, the grain would be sprouting rootlets and the beginnings of green shoots. The grain was then spread evenly on the floor to a depth of between three to six inches (75 to 150 mm) and worked, by turning the grain with wooden shovels or rakes, so that germination could proceed evenly. Wooden shovels were used because metal implements could cause sparks in the enclosed space of the malthouse and cause a fire. The depth of the grain on the working floor was determined by atmospheric conditions – the colder the weather the greater the depth. Over 8 to 15 days each batch of grain or 'piece' would be moved further along the floor towards the kiln. If the grain showed signs of drying out, it was sprinkled with water. The grain was ready for kilning when the rootlets had turned brown and the green shoots had grown half way up the corn – at least that was the method followed in Ware, although in other malting areas the shoots were allowed to grow longer.

Germination now had to be stopped or the grain would become more of a plant and begin to lose its sugar content. This was done on a kiln with a wire floor or perforated tiles through which passed the hot air from a fire or furnace below. Kilning was usually done in two stages – first to dry the grain with plenty of air passing through, then the draught was cut down and the temperature raised to effect the final 'curing' during which the

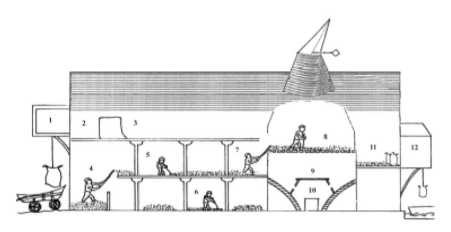

1. Hoist or lucam for the barley intake
2. Barley storage
3. Barley screen
4. Steeping cistern
5. Upper working floor
6. Lower working floor
7. Loading the kiln
8. Spreading on kiln floor
9. Iron fire bars or heat dispenser
10. Kiln furnace
11. Malt loft
12. Malt delivery by a lucam

*A typical floor malting, like the Southern Malting at Kibes Lane – based on the drawing by Sally Fraser in* 'Steeped in Tradition' *by Jonathan Brown (University of Reading, 1983).*

---

colour and flavour of the malt were determined.

When the Ware maltsters were making 'brown malt' for the porter brewers, the malt was 'high dried' – even scorched – at higher temperatures over furnaces burning hornbeam or oak. Coal was also used on kilns and in later years anthracite.

The finished malt was then stripped from the kiln and partially cooled in a malt loft before being moved to storage in the malt loft or in bins. As far as possible the malt was kept as dry as when it was on the kiln.

The malting season was traditionally from the beginning of September – after harvest – until Easter. In the summer the higher temperatures made it difficult to control germination of the grain.

*Above and below: Turning and levelling the germinating barley on a Ware malting floor.*

*A wooden screening machine for cleaning the grain and
(right) a kiln fire – both from the Hope Maltings in Baldock Street,
operated by Henry Ward & Sons.*

*Below: malting workers with a variety of tools at Henry Ward & Sons.*

# What gave Ware its importance in the malting trade?

In the eighteenth and nineteenth centuries Ware became the foremost supplier of malt to the London brewers. There were a number of reasons for this, the main ones being its:

- proximity to the barley-growing areas of East Anglia – Cambridgeshire, Suffolk, North Essex and North Hertfordshire;

- good transport links with London by the Old North Road and the River Lea, especially after construction of the Lee Navigation in 1760. These enabled malt to be delivered in bulk to London cheaply, and coal and foreign barley from London docks to be brought back to Ware. Delivery to London by barge went on even after the arrival of the railway;

- plentiful supply of hard, unpolluted water coming off the Chiltern hills;

- family and religious connections with the brewing trade in London, particularly with Quaker-owned breweries in Shoreditch and Southwark.

- Since malting was done in the winter, it provided an alternative occupation for workmen in the 'off season' of other industries, such as brickmaking.

- The importance of Ware as a coaching stop before the railways came, enabled brewers and their factors to visit the maltings and return to London the same day.

- In the early years there were plenty of large country houses in the vicinity requiring malt for brewing their own ale or beer.

# A 700-year tradition

Malting was not a monolithic industry – at least not until it became one in the late twentieth century. Traditionally there were three types of malting business. First, there were sales maltsters, selling their product to all comers. Before 1800 most towns and many villages had malthouses of this type where the big houses in the area could purchase malt for their brewing. Many of these sales maltsters were attached to the farms which grew the barley. Secondly, there were brewer maltsters, who malted barley for their own use. They too were common in the early years. Thirdly there were the commission maltsters, who were contracted to a large brewer to produce malt of a guaranteed quality and quantity, using the brewer's barley or alternatively buying the barley themselves. Commission maltsters became more common in the seventeenth century, especially in towns like Ware or Bishops Stortford which looked to London for their custom.

Malting in Ware is first recorded in 1307, when Robertus Maltus – Robert the maltster – had to pay 14¾ pence in taxes. In 1339 the bailiffs of Ware were ordered by the king to restore 12 quarters of malt* to Master Reymond Peregrini which had been confiscated by mistake. Master Peregrini had purchased the malt at Ware market for the use of a senior canon at St. Paul's Cathedral. The malt would have been produced by a sales maltster, either in Ware or nearby. At this period references to malting tend to occur only when someone goes to law or is arrested. In around 1470, the Steward of Ware arrested William Symmes, 'a common cariour of malte', who had been hired by one John Pratte to deliver 6 quarters of malt to William Whitehead, a brewer at Stratford-atte-Bow, who had refused it as 'not goode nor holesum for man'. Another case of 1510 involved Edward Wylson who sued John Archer of Ware for the balance of money due for 20 quarters of malt.

---

\* *Traditionally, malt was measured by volume or dry capacity rather than weight – a quarter consisting of 8 bushels. Later the bushel became a unit of weight: one bushel of barley = 48 lb or 21.77 kg.*

The relationship between country maltsters and their London brewery customers changed with the change of religion. Henry VIII's Dissolution of the Monasteries between 1536 and 1541 caused thousands of people to take to the roads seeking employment. The population of London grew so rapidly that it had doubled within ten years, putting the supply of corn and malt for bread and ale under great pressure. Queen Elizabeth's chief minister, William Cecil, Lord Burghley, set out to improve the water carriage of malt and corn by ordering the River Lea to be cleared of obstructions. This was a success, though not without resistance from Enfield traders who carried malt to London by pack horse. A return to the Middlesex Sessions in 1609 showed there were 34 barges working the Lea with capacities ranging from 26 to 42 quarters of malt or corn. There were 22 different barge owners – one from Braughing, two each from Broxbourne, Stanstead Abbots and Enfield, three each from Hertford, Waltham and London and six from Ware. One Ware owner, Richard Brooke, had two barges – the *Little Blue Lion* and the *Great Blue Lion*, which carried 42 quarters and was worked by five men.

'Unreasonable loads of malt'

The trade between Ware maltsters and the brewers of London was now well established. It would go on growing in importance for the next three centuries. But it had its down-side. In 1646-7 it was reported to the Hertfordshire Sessions that:

> the great decay of all the ways arises through the unreasonable loads of malt brought into and through Ware to Hodsdon from remote parts, and the bringing of great loads of malt from both the Hadhams, Alburie, Starford, all the Pelhams and Clavering, through Ware Extra* and the excessive loads from Norwich, Bury, and Cambridge weekly, the team often consisting of 7 or 8 horses. There is a great increase of maltsters in Ware.

* *Ware Extra (as distinct from 'Ware Infra') was the rural part of the parish including Wareside and Thundridge.*

*An eighteenth-century engraving of the turnpike at Wadesmill*
*– set up to control the malting traffic to and from Ware.*

The magistrates went on to suggest that if the maltsters carried lighter loads with only four horses 'as they used to', the roads would sustain less damage. As far back as 1636, restraints on malting were introduced in Stortford, Hitchin, Baldock, Ashwell and Royston – but not in Ware. The upshot of this concern about the burgeoning malting industry was the establishment in 1663 of a turnpike on the Old North Road north of Ware at Wadesmill. The intention of the Act of Parliament had been to establish three toll gates on the road – the others would have been at Caxton in Cambridgeshire and Stilton in Huntingdon – but the only one erected was at Wadesmill. Inevitably there were complaints from road users and also from the Ware innkeepers who said that the daily toll discouraged carriers from staying overnight. But the author, Daniel Defoe, gave a better account of the road between Royston and Ware:

> though this road is continually work'd upon, by reason of the vast number of Carriages, bringing Malt and Barley to Ware, for whose sake indeed it was obtained; yet, with small repairs it is maintain'd and the Toll is reduced from a penny to a halfpenny.

Elsewhere in his 1724 *Tour thro' the Whole Island of Great Britain* Defoe said that the fields of Hertfordshire were given over to barley, generally sold to Ware and Royston and is 'the fund from whence that vast quantity of malt, call'd Hertfordshire malt, is made which is esteem'd the best in England'.

15

# Brown malt and porter

In 1722 or perhaps before, there occurred an event which changed the drinking habits of Londoners and added to the fortunes of Ware's maltsters. It was the creation of the beer known as 'porter'. It is an event shrouded in mystery, and so it should be for it was the inauguration of a wonderful beverage. Before 1722 London brewers had been producing a sweetish, amber-coloured ale that quickly lost its strength, so that it became common practice for publicans to mix old and new ales or to draw a pint from three different casks – one of beer, another of ale (i.e. beer without hops) and the third from more expensive pale ale, commonly known as 'two-penny'. That meant that every pint served in London consisted of at least one third flat beer. Ralph Harwood, a partner in the Bell Brewhouse in Shoreditch, overcame that problem by brewing a beer which was strong, dark and bitter and, above all, kept its strength – in fact, it was best drunk when it was several weeks or months old. Because it overcame the problem of the different casks, he called it 'Entire' or 'Entire Butt'. But because it was so popular with London's labourers it soon became known as 'porter'. Because it kept its strength, it was the first beer that was suitable for mass production by the common brewers, and soon all the major London brewers were switching from pale and amber beers to the darker porter. It was through porter that the Calvert family at the Hour Glass Brewery beside the Thames were able to increase production to 50,000 and then 100,000 barrels a year.

What gave porter its colour and special taste was that it was brewed from a special brown malt, which was 'high dried', that is cured over a very hot kiln fire of oak or hornbeam faggots rather than coal. Whether or not brown malt was first discovered in Ware, it soon became a speciality of the Ware maltsters. It was not a particularly high quality malt, in fact it was made from poorer quality barleys and this was welcome because it gave porter a price advantage. The main features of 'Ware Brown' were its taste and its colour which gave porter its flavour – and its consistency. These features depended on the skills of the Ware maltsters for without them the heat of the wood-burning kiln could as easily produce scorched or even roasted malt. As an anonymous article in 1736 in the *London and Country Brewer* magazine, put it:

> I have heard a great Malster that lived towards *Ware*, say, he knew a grand Brewer, that wetted near two hundred Quarters a Week, was not a judge of good and bad Malts, without which 'tis impossible to draw a true length of Ale or Beer. To do this I know but few ways. *First*, by the Bite, is to break the Malt-Corn across between the Teeth, in the middle of it or at both Ends, and if it tasteth mellow and sweet, has a round Body, breaks soft, is full of flower all its length, smells well and has a thin skin, then it is good; *Secondly*, by Water; to take a Glass near full, and put in some Malt; and if it swims, it is right, but if any sinks to the bottom, then it is not true Malt, but steely and retains somewhat of its Barley nature.

It used to be said in Ware that a maltster needed good teeth – to be able to chew the new malt and spit it on to the hand to test its colour and quality. Because the major brewers so much trusted the consistency of 'Ware Brown' malt, it acquired its own premium price at the corn market in Mark Lane, London. There were well-documented instances of Suffolk and Norfolk barley, which would normally be made into malt there, being shipped as barley to London, then sent in the malt barges to Ware as 'back carriage' so that it gained from the Ware maltsters' skills and their premium price[1]. As far as brown malt was concerned, the London brewers distinctly preferred the Ware product, but not so with the pale malts where all the Hertfordshire maltsters faced stiff – and increasing – competition from Norfolk and from the Surrey maltsters who shipped their malt from Kingston-on-Thames.

---

[1] Peter Mathias, *TheBrewing Industry in England, 1700-1830* (Cambridge University Press, 1959), 439 – quoting evidence to a parliamentary commission

# The Lee Navigation

Since Lord Burghley's initiative in Elizabeth's reign, the River Lea had been the main route for getting Hertfordshire malt to the London brewers. But it was not a greatly different waterway from that of the Middle Ages. There was no efficient tow-path for horse-drawn barges and there were few 'pound locks' with gates to cope with falls in the river – as a result each miller or weir-owner on the route had to be paid for a 'flash' of water to get the barge past the obstruction. The river greatly needed to be managed and improved by one authority rather than having piecemeal efforts to remove obstacles.

The first steps were taken by an Act of Parliament of 1739, which established a body of Trustees and gave them a modest income. This was a grant of £3,250 and £350 p.a. as rent from the New River Company for the water it was extracting from the Lea – at that time by means of a 'balance engine' on the old 'barge river' on the Meads. New pound locks were provided at Ware, Stanstead Abbotts and Broxbourne, but more radical improvements were needed. In 1765 the Trustees commissioned a survey from the engineer John Smeaton, who reported that there were eighteen major obstacles between Ware and the Thames which should be replaced by pound locks. He also proposed a number of new cuts to straighten and canalise the river. Despite some opposition from bodies lower down river, a new Act of Parliament in 1767 gave the Trustees powers to improve the navigation and to raise tolls to pay for improvements and maintenance. As a result many straight cuts or canals were created, like that between Ware and Stanstead Abbotts; another local improvement was to make the millstream to Ware Mill into part of the Navigation, thus doing away with the winding 'barge river' over the Meads. But the most welcome improvement for the bargemen and their skippers was a new entry of the Lea into the Thames. This was the Limehouse Cut which enabled barges to avoid the tidal Bow Creek and the long passage around the Isle of Dogs. The route was further shortened by new channels at Cheshunt, Hackney and Old Ford.

The first meeting of the Lee Trustees was held at the Crown

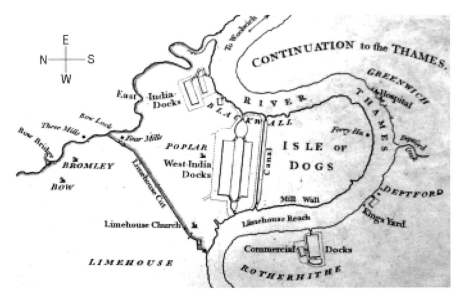

*John Smeaton's drawing of the lower part of the Lee Navigation,*
*showing the Limehouse Cut which avoided Bow Creek*
*and the long journey around the Isle of Dogs.*

Inn in Ware on August 6, 1739, attended by (among others) the brewers Felix and Peter Calvert of Furneaux Pelham and Rivers Dickinson of Ware, and the maltsters Zacheus Haydon and John Kemp. Later meetings were held in various inns along the river, including the Bull in Ware since the Crown Inn was demolished in 1765. London brewers, especially those with Hertfordshire connections, were again well represented – including David Barclay of Wadesmill. The Ware maltsters on the Trust included Daniel Adams, Andrew Searle, John Kemp and John Scott who, like David Barclay, was a Quaker. Another Quaker, Sampson Hanbury of Poles near Ware who owned Truman's Brewery in Shoreditch, became a Trustee in 1800. Others represented on the Trust were the MPs of Hertfordshire and Essex, Aldermen of the City of London and some of the banks.

In October 1769 the improvements in the Lea as far as Ware were extended north-east to Bishop's Stortford by canalising the River Stort for navigation. This was the key to the development of Stortford and later Sawbridgeworth as major malting centres, to which some of the Ware maltsters soon moved.

# Ware and the Excise

In the days before Income Tax – introduced by William Pitt as a 'war tax' against the French – the greater part of Britain's Exchequer came from Excise duties and taxes. Beer and malt were regarded as prime commodities to be taxed. There had been a duty on beer since 1643 and its proceeds went some way to financing the Civil War. A similar duty on malt had been considered for many years and was finally introduced in 1697 at the height of a war against France. Some people maintained that in the interests of social justice the beer duty should have been abolished at the same time, but this was not done.

To avoid the problem of surveying private houses, people making malt for family consumption were allowed to compound for a modest annual figure. Commercial maltsters, like those in Ware, had to pay a duty of $6^{16}/_{21}$d. (six and sixteen-twenty-firsts pence) per bushel. As Britain found itself engaged in later wars, the malt duty was increased to 9¼d. per bushel in 1760, to 1s.4¼d. in 1780, to 1s.7¾d. in 1791 and to a phenomenal 4s.5¾d. in 1803 during the Napoleonic War, then reduced to 2s.5d. in 1816 after the Battle of Waterloo. Malt and corn were always measured by their volume rather than weight – a bushel (roughly 0.036 cubic metres) was the standard measure and there were eight bushels to a quarter. A contemporary manuscript reported that in 1788 there were 33 maltings in Ware, employing 70 men and producing 1,370 quarters of malt per week during the season (October to March). That is a great deal of malt on its way to London, and represents 372,640 bushels during the season and an annual payment of malt duty by the Ware maltsters of £25,230. That was quite a considerable sum for a small town, not counting what it contributed in land tax, beer duty or duties on coal, brandy, etc. Since the total national excise revenue was only £6.75 million, the Ware maltsters would have been providing something like 0.37 % of the national revenue. Every 370th frigate or Hussite mercenary – or musket or grenade – in the war against the Americans and French was paid for by the Ware malt tax. According to the trade directories, the Ware maltsters were paying £120,000 in duty in 1838 and £200,000 in 1869.

These figures go some way to explaining the seriousness with which the Government took the events in Ware in 1787-88. Liability for the malt duty was based on measurements made by the Excise before the germination process began – excisemen would go to the malthouse of a licensed maltster and measure the 'couched' or piled-up barley with their rules and gauges. To combat cheating, such as hiding or compressing the barley, strict regulations were introduced throughout the century. By the end of the century there were almost 100 different rules and penalties, with the result that a continual struggle took place between Excise officers enforcing the law and artful maltsters finding ways of evading the regulations to produce a proportion of duty-fee malt.

In 1787, a new Supervisor of the Excise, named Robert Grand, arrived in Ware and immediately tried to enforce the regulations by taking maltsters to court. His first efforts failed when the magistrates at the Hertford Quarter Sessions (who no doubt had their own interests in the industry) threw out all of Grand's prosecutions. "This conduct of the excise officers made them obnoxious to the people," reported two of the local gentry, "who have hallooed and hooted them but never assaulted or obstructed them in the execution of their duty". On the 24 September 1788, Grand and two of his excisemen, one of them named Veal, went to inspect the malting stock of Worrall, a tallow chandler, and were hooted at by a crowd that had gathered. There was no other obstruction apart from "a little street dirt thrown at them".

But Grand complained to the Commisioners of Excise who arranged with the War Office for a troop of cavalry to enter the town. Grand went to the Bull Inn to meet a group of maltsters assembled there and insisted on having a military escort. A commotion ensued. The town constables refused to issue warrants against the maltsters and demanded of the cavalry's commanding officer by whose authority he had come into the town. He answered that he had come at the request of Supervisor Grand. Alarm then spread throughout the town with the result that there was a down-tools in the malthouses and only four of the 33 maltings were in operation. The Vicar and the two Nonconformist ministers organised a petition which they passed to the county magistrates and Members of Parliament, who concluded that the Ware people "had been extremely ill used". Eventually, the case came before the Chancellor of the Exchequer, William Pitt, who resolved the matter by removing Mr Grand from Ware [2].

The London brewers favoured Hertfordshire malts, especially Ware Brown, and so towards the end of the eighteenth century did the Excise. In Ware, Hertford and Bishop's Stortford, the barley was steeped in a cistern and then laid on the malting floor, where it was turned continuously but never wetted again. This method was suitable for barley grown on the light soils of Hertfordshire and East Anglia. Barleys grown from heavier soils in other parts of the country were reluctant to germinate and yield up their enzymes, with the result that the maltster would wet or sprinkle the grains after a few days on the malting floor to spur on germination. This the excisemen disliked. It made it possible for an unscrupulous maltster to add newly-sprinkled barley to the stock which had already been measured for tax purposes. And so in 1802, Parliament passed an Act banning the sprinkling of barley which had already been assessed. It caused uproar in the rest of the country.

> The law was clearly in the interests of the Hertfordshire maltsters (who did not sprinkle) and the London brewers, who were enabled to force all their competitors to compete with them on their own terms of manufacture without their advantages of developed skill [3].

Protest meetings were held in the West Country, the Midlands and south of the Thames. A committee of maltsters from these parts lobbied Parliament, which set up its own investigation. Despite witnesses from the Excise and Hertfordshire, Cambridgeshire and Essex, the prohibition was scrapped and in 1806 sprinkling was again permitted after a certain number of days had elapsed.

---

[2] Royal Commission on Historical Manuscripts, Earl of Verulam at Gorhambury, 133, 136-8.

[3] Peter Mathias, *op. cit*, 410.

# Friends and Maltfactors

One advantage Ware and Hertfordshire maltsters enjoyed over their rivals was their friendly and family relationships with the major brewers of London. Many of the latter came from Hertfordshire anyway – the Dickinsons from Ware, Sir William Calvert and Felix Calvert from Furneaux Pelham, Ralph and Henry Thrale from St. Albans. When Henry Thrale died in 1771 and left the Anchor Brewery in Southwark on the verge of bankruptcy, Mrs Thrale was left to pick up the pieces with the help of Dr. Johnson. Promptly, Mrs Hankin, the mother of a Ware maltfactor, loaned Mrs Thrale the sum of £6,000. A little later, David Barclay of Youngsbury at Wadesmill, went into partnership with the Thrales' manager, John Perkins, and bought out Mrs Thrale to form the brewery company of Barclay, Perkins & Co.

One of the closest relationships was that between the brewer, Sampson Hanbury – who incidentally was married to David Barclay's granddaughter – and the Hertfordshire maltsters. Sampson Hanbury acquired an interest in the Black Eagle Brewery in Brick Lane, Spitalfields, in 1780 on the death of Sir Benjamin Truman, and in 1789 assumed full control with the Truman family as sleeping partners. In 1800, probably because of his wife's connections with the area, Sampson Hanbury took out a lease on Poles, a large country house on the Ware side of Thundridge, and in 1820 bought the house and lived there until his death in 1835. Sampson and his wife had no children so the house – and a partnership in the brewery – went to his nephew, Robert Hanbury. In the meantime, in 1808 Sampson had taken into partnership another nephew, Thomas Fowell Buxton, the son of his sister Anna. This Buxton, who later became an M.P. and was associated with William Wilberforce in the campaign to abolish the slave trade, gave his name to the firm which then became known as Truman, Hanbury, Buxton & Co. His son, another Thomas Fowell Buxton, bought the Easnye estate at Stanstead Abbots while the Hanburys continued to live at Poles. The firm were mainly porter brewers and Sampson Hanbury bought his brown malt from Ware – though increasingly the pale malt came from elsewhere in East Anglia – all the while acting through the skilled intermediaries known as maltfactors.

Maltfactors were the key middlemen in the brewer/maltster relationships of the late eighteenth century. They gained an important role because the London brewers now required large quantities of malt and could not produce this themselves. So the factors collected samples

*Sampson Hanbury (1769-1835)*
*from a portrait by Sir Martin Archer Shree*

from a number of maltings, delivered these to the brewers, held stocks of malt, distributed payment, granted credit and – in many cases – delivered the malt in their own barges to London. Sampson Hanbury employed three main factors: in Ware there was William Adams, in Bishop's Stortford John Taylor, and in Essex and the rest of East Anglia John Kemp. John Taylor was the son of Samuel Taylor, a barge-owner and maltster who had bought a small property beside Ware Bridge in 1786, about the same time John had moved to Stortford with the opening up of the Stort Navigation. These Taylors were ancestors of the prominent Sawbridgeworth firm of maltsters, H.A.& D. Taylor Ltd. The main point here is that John Taylor's relationship with Sampson Hanbury went beyond business affairs. They were close personal friends and Taylor would visit Hanbury's in-laws, the Gurney family, when he visited Norfolk. William Adams was a member of the family which was prominent in barge-owning, malting and later banking in the town for over a hundred years. In 1809, William was the main factor for the new Meux Reid brewery and in the summer of 1814 was holding stock of malt in Ware valued at £22,000.

A little later similar friendships existed between another Ware maltster, Edward Chuck, and members of the Courage and Whitbread families to whose breweries he supplied malt. Edward Chuck was godfather to Edward Courage, who joined the Courage Brewery in Southwark in 1854 and later became a partner. And when Edward Chuck died, W.H. Whitbread, head of the brewery in Chiswell Street in the City of London, came down to Ware to attend the funeral. The life of Edward Chuck (1783-1852) well illustrates the steps by which many Ware maltsters rose to prominence, progressing through family links and business opportunities, some of which must have seemed dead ends at the time. His grandfather had been a publican who was engaged in maltmaking in a small way and his father a maltster. Edward's wife, Elizabeth, also came from a Ware malting family. But malting was not Edward's only or even his main occupation at first. From 1819 until 1826, he was a partner in the Ware Bank with George Cass, his father-in-law, and John Cass, his brother-in-law. For much of the same period he was a partner with Thomas Meakin and John King in a wholesale lead and glass business in London. He seems to have owned a lead mine and, in later years, he was an active farmer in the four farmsteads he owned to the north of Ware. The one in which he lived, Noah's Ark Farm, may well have been named after Edward's hobby of breeding superior livestock. Before Aline Burgess did research into her family of Collins (related to the Chuck, Page and Croft families), Edward Chuck was not fully recognised as the important maltster he was. Now it can be seen that he was a vital piece in the jigsaw of relationships between the pioneering maltsters of the eighteenth century and the large-scale, industrial maltsters of the nineteenth.

The memorial in St. Mary's to his in-laws, the Cass family, shows that George Cass senior, 'Late of this Town, Maltfactor' died in 1826, aged 74 years, while Edward's successor – and relative by marriage – Henry Page, died in 1892, leaving more than a million pounds, all earned from making malt. Edward Chuck left his mark on the town in many ways. The colourful east window of St. Mary's was a memorial to his parents while his own memorial (apart from the tomb in the old burial ground off Church Street) was the grammar school his widow built at the top of Musley Hill. He also lived in and greatly expanded No. 87 High Street (now Ware Library) which later became the home of Henry Page and his daughter, Mrs Anne E. Croft.

*Edward Chuck (1783-1852)*
*by Sir Francis Grant PRA*

Maltfactors were regarded as the gentlemen of the malting industry. Usually they were former maltsters who had given up the hands-on business of making malt to act as middle men for the brewing companies. As such, they were usually wealthy in their own right and able to finance deals with the maltsters on behalf of brewers who would often not pay their bills until many months later. Many maltfactors celebrated the change of status by moving their residence upmarket. Samuel Adams, who was also a banker, acquired the Cannons Mansion in Baldock Street;  Charles Cass in 1864 built the Presdales Mansion, later the home of the Sandeman and McMullen families and now a school.  But malting was not always a guaranteed route to wealth and comfort.  In 1857, William Cater described as a maltster and maltfactor, formerly of the High Street, Ware, then of the Rectory (the present Manor House) appeared before a judge at Hertford County Court as a bankrupt. It seems that his woes had begun with a fire in his malting. Before his court appearance, he had been kept in Hertford gaol.

# New sources of competition

In the early years of the nineteenth century, the dominance of Ware malt among the big common brewers of London was threatened from many sides. The Ware entry in Pigot's Directory for 1832 could confidently state that "most of the London breweries are supplied from this town" but things were changing fast. There was fierce competition from the maltsters of Norfolk and Suffolk, who took their malt to the Port of London by ship, and from those of Kingston-on-Thames and farther west, who shipped their malt to the capital by barge. Norfolk and Kingston Pale malts could now compete in both quality and price with the best Hertfordshire Pale. Matters were made worse by a rapid succession of other issues: the slump in grain prices following the end of the wars with France, the Beer Act of 1830 (which abolished the duty on beer but did not affect the malt tax) and the repeal of the Corn Laws which allowed barley imports from France, Denmark and Germany.

These issues greatly increased the competition for the types of malt used in brewing pale ale, but Ware Brown malt for porter brewing was still holding its own. The reason is that the Ware maltsters and the London porter brewers had a classic symbiotic relationship. The brewers required their Hertfordshire suppliers to make malt, in which germinating barley produced a shoot – or acrospire – of a half to three-quarters the length of the grain: the London brewers because of their efficient production were able to extract more sugar from this 'short-grown malt', so that is what they ordered. On the other hand, at Newark in the Trent Valley and other parts of Britain away from Hertfordshire, the germinating barley was allowed to develop an acrospire from three-quarters to the whole length of the grain. This was achieved by liberal sprinkling of the grains and this gave them a greater degree of modification of the starch into sugar. The Ware maltsters and their backers castigated the others for 'forcing' – the Newark maltsters, on the other hand, knew a thing or two that the Ware maltsters were unaware of.

The danger came not from Newark but from farther up the valley at Burton-on-Trent. Even before the coming of the

*Brown malt kilns built in the 1840s – backing on to the Buryfields although accessed from Baldock Streeet.*

railways, the relatively small brewing industry of Burton had made its mark on the worldwide economy through its production of India Pale Ale for export via the port of Liverpool. IPA was a brew quite different from London porter: it was a heavily-hopped, strong and bitter pale ale, well able to keep its strength which was necessary in view of the long sea voyage to India. The water of Burton was found to be particularly good for IPA. There soon developed a British market for IPA which received an enormous boost with the arrival of the railways. Having a brewery only a few horse-drawn miles from its customers was no longer vital. As Burton firms like Bass and Allsop expanded, breweries in other parts of the country with water similar to Burton's started making their own versions of IPA. However, the London brewers did not have this advantage and so began to open their own breweries in Burton. From 1835 to 1870, most of the London porter brewers – including Truman, Hanbury and Buxton – opened their own brewhouses at Burton.

But that was not the only change. As brewers around the country competed with the IPA of Burton so they produced variations of it. Pale ales became less heavily-hopped, with a lighter, brighter appearance and more sparkle. They had a shorter life and were supplied in bottles. Thus porter now had two rivals: India Pale Ale from Burton and bottled Light Ale from many different locations.

These were major threats to the dominance of Ware Brown malt and they caused widespread changes. Throughout the town, older and often small, one-man malthouses were demolished and replaced with brick maltings of two or three floors, with larger kilns. Many of these new maltings were designed for the production of high quality pale malts and they had kilns fired by coal or anthracite rather than wood, but brown malt was also being produced – there was still a market for it. It was a period of technological innovation. Ware had long had a modest engineering industry: from the seventeenth century onwards Welsh ironmasters had seen the sense in having a base within easy reach of London by river. Now, in the late 1830s, with the arrival of the railways, engineering know-how was put into the service of the malting industry. One of the innovators was Charles Wells, with premises behind Nos.49-51 High Street, which in earlier times had been the Bear Inn and earlier still the Falcon. According to an illustrated feature in *The Pictorial Record* of January 1899, the Falcon Works was started by Charles Wells over a century earlier and carried on by him until his death in about 1860, when it was acquired by A.J. Goodfellow. It was an extensive works, with a large smith's shop, five fires, a farriers' shop "for shoeing horses on scientific principles", an engineering shop with steam-driven plant, a foundry and a wire-working department. Commenting on the wire-working department, the feature said:

> this latter forms one of the chief specialities of the business, and in almost every malt-producing county Messrs. A.J. Goodfellow & Co.'s malt kiln wire floors are widely used; the same applying to their own malting cowls. They have made a study of this class of work and have now a widespread reputation for it. In addition to the home trade, a good deal of work in this line is also done for export.

In earlier periods, kiln floors had been made of wood, of wrought-iron bars or ceramic tiles. The Wells-Goodfellow innovation was to produce floors with a fine wire mesh, suspended on wrought-iron rods running laterally across the

*One of the revolving kiln cowls and (right) a tie plate*
*to secure the iron rods which supported the wire floor of the kiln*
*– both from the Southern Malting at Kibes Lane and both*
*manufactured by Charles Wells at the Falcon Iron Works.*

building and held tense by wrought-iron tie-plates on the outside of the kiln. In Ware these tie-plates have the distinction of bearing the manufacturer's name, Charles Wells, the Goodfellow family or other smiths from Ware and Hertford. The recording and rescue of these tie-plates was a special interest of the late Michael Ottley who gave a number to the Ware Museum.

Because these technologically new malt-kilns could stand very high temperatures, it was more necessary than ever that the kiln fumes and steam should be evacuated as rapidly as possible to prevent the danger of fire. Hence the work of the Falcon Works on their own malting cowls, which were of conical shape and able to swivel away from the wind and thus prevent any blow-back. They were a great improvement on older kiln cowls of a 'mortar-board' design. A typical pair of these malting cowls, and also the wire floors and tie-plates, can be found at the Southern Malting in New Road/Kibes Lane, which was one of three parallel maltings built in the 1840s. Charles Wells's tie plates also exist on the kiln of the Middle Malting. Other examples of these 1840s brick maltings can be found in the former Crook Brothers yard off Watton Road.

Ware malt was now holding its own, but not much more than that. With the coming of the railways, particularly the Great Northern Railway, the London brewers were able to draw supplies of malt from centres like Grantham, Lincoln and Newark. As a result the importance of the Ware market began to decline. One indication of this is that during the 1870s the newspapers ceased quoting special rates for Ware-made malt and the number of firms in Ware began to decline. Yet the output of the town was still considerable. The two major firms, Henry Page & Co. and Hudson and Ward (later Henry Ward & Sons), each operated a number of malthouses in Ware, Hertford and Bishop's Stortford – producing respectively 55,000 and 35,000 quarters a year. But there were many maltsters which far exceeded that output in other parts of the country.

## Malting becomes an industry

The second half of the nineteenth century saw great changes in the malting industry in Ware. The prosperity of Victorian Britain and its Empire around the world meant there was a growing market for beer and ale of all varieties, and consequently for malt. New people entered the business, some with the capital and connections immediately to become maltsters, while others chanced their luck with smaller resources after an apprenticeship as a steersman or barge-owner. In 1869 – according to the sanitation engineers, Russ and Minns – it was estimated that the population of Ware had grown to nearly 7,000 and the town contained "the largest malting establishments in the world" with an annual production of nearly two million bushels.

By 1880 there were well over a hundred malthouses in the town, many with more than one kiln. Every spare plot of land had been taken over by maltings, coloured as a sea of pink on one copy of the 1880 Ordnance Survey Map. Gradually these maltings and their kilns were passing into the control of a handful of major malting families. The Post Office Directory of 1862 listed the main maltsters as John and Samuel Adams on Musley Hill, Charles Cass and Joseph and Silas Chuck in Baldock Street, John Cowell in Crib Street, James Collyer, William Hudson, Henry Page, George Thorowgood, Isaac Waller and Samuel Wright, all in the High Street and Henry Edward Green in Star Street. By 1882, John Adams and John Cowell were still working, joined by two other single maltsters, Caleb Hitch in Star Street and Thomas Chapman in New Road. But all the others were now malting companies – the Cambridgeshire maltsters Thoday Ingle Few & Co. in Baldock Street, Chidley, Phillips & Co. in New Road; and Croft & Co., Joseph Gripper & Sons, Hudson & Ward and Henry Page & Co. in High Street. The Gripper family were originally Quakers who had taken over the Dickinson family's malthouses behind East Street in the 1740s. The firm of Hudson & Ward was the result of a marriage between two dynasties but sadly their offspring and hope for the future, Henry Hudson Ward, was killed fighting in the South African war as a cavalry lieutenant in February 1902 (his name is on the memorial in St. Mary's).

The greatest of these malting entrepreneurs was Henry Page. His father had been a part-time maltster, corn-dealer and baker in Churchgate House (Jacoby's Restaurant) in West Street. It was later well-known as the bakery of Jaggs and Edward's. In the 1830s, Henry married Anne Collins, niece of the maltster Edward Chuck, and on Edward's death in 1852 he acquired most of his uncle-in-law's malthouses. It was a contentious sharing out of the family assets which saw other maltings going to Joseph Chuck and his son, Silas. The dispute may have had something to do with religion, for the late Edward Chuck, his sister Susanna Collins and nephew-in-law, Henry Page (who had begun life as a Quaker) were all faithful members of St. Mary's, the Parish Church, while the brother Joseph Chuck was a member and benefactor of the Congregational Church (Leaside). Henry Page was a skilled maltster and a first-rate businessman. Despite losing one fortune in the collapse of Samuel Adams's Ware Bank in 1856, he went on building his business and rising up the social scale. In its heyday, the firm of Henry Page & Co. owned forty maltings in Ware and Hertford.

In 1880, the Liberal government announced abolition of the malt tax which did not please Henry Page. On 16 July 1880, he wrote the following letter:

To      The Right Honourable W.E. Gladstone, Chancellor of the Exchequer and First Lord of the Treasury

Honourable Sir,

This morning I have read in The Times paper "that it was for those who desired a continuance of the Duty on ready-made Malt imported into the United Kingdom, to shew cause for it, as the Duty on Malt was being abolished." May I, Sir, say a few words on this subject?

I for one, Sir, strongly object to the total withdrawal of that Import Duty. The Maltsters ought to have some security of the value of their maltings. I have under the supervision of the Excise Officers, and in entire accordance with the Law at the time, in constructing my maltings, been put to great expense which I should not have incurred had not that Law been in force. I think I ought to claim some sort of remuneration knowing as I did, that the Import Duty on foreign Malt gave me some security on building and buying Maltings to the extent of forty, which I hold in the town of Ware. I believe that single-handed I pay more Duty than any other Maltster.

I should, Sir, have applied to my friend the Honourable Henry Cowper for his assistance in this matter but did not know whether he was in England, and I feared to lose time.

I am Honoured Sir,
Always yours faithfully and obediently,
(Signed) Henry Page

The Hon. Henry Cowper was one of the MPs for Hertfordshire and, like Henry Page, a Liberal.

*Henry Page (1812-94)*
*a photograph taken by his son-in-law, Richard Benyon Croft*

Gladstone's legislation – popularly known as the 'Free Mash Tun' Act – transferred the tax from malt to beer, thus enabling brewers to use any variety of malt or substitute ingredients in their mash. But abolition of the malt tax also changed maltmaking. Freed from the hundreds of Excise regulations about measuring barley in the cistern, couch-frame or on the malting floor, maltsters were now able to redesign their malthouses and introduce mechanisation. They were able also to use imported barley from Europe – or even barley substitute if the British harvest was bad. The impetus for change was helped by the steady increase in beer production in England and Wales from 27 million barrels in 1880 to almost 32 million barrels in 1990 with a corresponding increase in the demand for malt.

The first Ware maltster to take advantage of the new freedoms was Hudson Ward & Co. which built new brick malting floors in their home yard behind 63 High Street, with a four-storey kiln. The brickwork carried the date 1885 along with the initials of the partners of the business – F.E.W., W.S.W. Similar tall kilns were built throughout the town – see the next page. Henry Page & Co. built their biggest malthouse and kiln in Star Street to celebrate Queen Victoria's Golden Jubilee in 1887, but it burned down in 1906. In its place, they built the much larger Victoria Maltings at Broadmeads in 1908 and closed many of their smaller malthouses at the same time. This too burned down in 1988.

*Four malt kilns built in the 1880s after abolition of the Malt Tax –*
*top row: behind 63 High Street for Hudson Ward & Co.*
*and in Star Street for Caleb Hitch & Son ;*
*bottom row: the Buryfield Maltings for James Hudson*
*and in Hoe Lane for Charles Cass.*

# The twentieth century

The Ware maltsters entered the new century in a spirit of optimism. In the early years, demand for beer and therefore for malt continued to rise, despite a hike in the beer tax to help pay for the South African or Boer War. Improvements in rail and road transport enabled Ware maltsters to reduce their dependence a little on the London brewers – the new customers of Henry Page & Co. included Showell's brewery in Birmingham and Crosswell's Cardiff Brewery.

The company showed their optimism by constructing a cathedral-sized malthouse at Broadmeads in 1908. This was the new Victoria Maltings, in its time the biggest and most modern in Britain, although it was soon overtaken by even larger maltings. It had a capacity of 200 qrs., five storeys of malting floors and many modern and progressive methods, such as self-emptying steeps and mechanised moving of grain, then found in

*The Victoria Maltings – built by Henry Page & Co. in 1908, taken out of commission in 1965 and burned down in 1988.*

*In its time, the Victoria Maltings was the tallest building in Ware –
dominating the town like a cathedral. The photograph above shows the
view across the bridge in the 1940s, with the Victory pub
(known as 'The Ship') on the left at the top of Amwell End.
Below is the large barley store which faced on the river, and
the footbridge across the Cut.*

very few maltings in Britain. In 1909 Henry Page & Co. became a Private Limited Company with registered capital of £125,000. The first chairman was Richard Benyon Croft – son-in-law of the founder, Henry Page – and the board included his two sons Col. Richard Page Croft and Col. Henry Page Croft, with Mr H.J. Buckmaster as managing director. Henry Page & Co. was emerging as one of the market leaders, producing around 100,000 quarters of malt annually. A table of production in 1913 shows the company ranked eighth in Britain, behind mainly East Anglia maltsters and just behind H.A. & D. Taylor of Sawbridgeworth.

However, maltsters who did not rank as market leaders did not always share this optimism. William S. Ward, of Henry Ward & Sons, wrote to a colleague in 1914 that "selling matches … could easily be more profitable than trying to sell malt"[4]. One can see what William had in mind when one looks at the firm's profit figures for the years before the First World War. From 1902-04, Ward & Sons made net profits of around £6,000 on capital of £34,600, but in 1905-06 profits dipped to around £4,500 and, having climbed again in 1907-09, they dipped to £3,249 in 1910 and £2,909 in 1911[5]. The problem was two-fold. Not being a market leader meant that Ward's unlike Henry Page & Co. could not compete for the best brewery contracts or, having less capital, take advantage of 'economies of scale'. The other problem was that wage costs were rising. For most of the second half of the nineteenth century, the wages paid to labourers in maltings had remained stable at 18s. to 22s. a week, but by 1906 labourers' wages were on the increase from 24s to 26s. And by the 1930s, wages in some parts of the malting industry, such as the Bass brewery maltings at Burton-on-Trent, were as high as 71s. (£3.11s). Henry Ward & Sons delayed becoming a limited company until the worst of the thirties had passed, registering eventually in 1935 with capital of £55,000.

---

[4]    Hertfordshire Archives (HALS) D/EWd B20 –
        letter of 8 December 1914 to C. Long.
[5]    Quoted by Jonathan Brown, *Steeped in Tradition, the Malting Industry in Britain since the railway age* (University of Reading, 1983), 47.

# War and its aftermath

The First World War had a major impact on the malting industry from the very beginning, With its new powers granted under the Defence of Realm Act in August 1914, the government imposed strict controls on both malting and brewing. The supply of barley and hops was tightly controlled, particularly since cereal imports were under constant attack by German submarines. Even more severe were the shackles imposed on brewers, which went far beyond what most people regarded as reasonable.

There existed a strong prejudice against the industry – summed up in the famous remark by David Lloyd George, Chancellor of the Exchequer, that "we are fighting Germany, Austria and Drink; as far as I can see, the greatest of these three deadly foes is Drink". In November 1914 the duty on a barrel of beer was increased from 7s.9d to 23s and by 1920 stood at 100s (£5). Beer production was limited and the strength of a pint decreased to match the new standard, the 'Government Ale': there was even a law that the person who buys beer must be the drinker – to stop people buying rounds. Worst of all were government moves towards nationalising the brewing industry, beginning with the 'Carlisle Experiment' in June 1916. Then the newly formed Central Control Board took control of five local breweries and 363 licensed premises in and around the city of Carlisle – 'for the duration of the war and 12 months thereafter' – in order to curb alleged drunkenness at a nearby munitions factory. In addition, there was the growing shortage of labour, as malting workers were conscripted into the Armed Forces and maltsters failed to persuade the government that maltmaking was a 'reserved occupation'. The remedy for that was two-fold: to extend the malting season into the summer months so that fewer workers worked longer, and to recruit women. Women certainly worked in the Ware malthouses between 1914 and 1919 and for a few years afterwards.

Some malting firms went to the wall during the war, but for the majority the First World War and the brief post-war boom saw them not only surviving but increasing their profits. There were a number of reasons for this: government controls also meant lower costs and there was a trend towards diversification from malt-for-brewing into malted foods, malt extract and malt flour. There were instances of malting firms hiring out their barges – quite lucratively – to the government for the transport of men and munitions to the ports of Northern France. But in the longer term, the problems created by the war were to make the outlook for the malting industry distinctly gloomy. During the war many breweries found it easier and cheaper to make their own malt and the sales maltsters, like those in Ware, suffered accordingly.

The most serious long-term problem for malting was the fall in beer production because of a fall in beer consumption. A whole generation of young men, who would normally have been the breweries' best customers, had been wiped out. The old community pub of Victorian times was disappearing. With the increase in beer duty and changing attitudes towards leisure and family life, the crowded public bar was becoming far less crowded. In 1922 most malting companies were thought to be working at about half their capacity and matters became progressively worse as the Twenties progressed. Kelly's Directory for Hertfordshire in 1929 showed that the number of working maltsters in Ware had fallen from eleven to four, all of whom were now companies – J. Harrington & Son in Coronation Road and High Street, Caleb Hitch & Son in Star Street, Henry Page & Co Ltd. at 85 High Street and Henry Ward & Sons, in Baldock Street and at 63 High Street.

In March 1932, a survey was made of fifty malting companies and its results were presented to the Chancellor of the Exchequer, Neville Chamberlain, by Sir Henry Page Croft MP, chairman of Henry Page & Co. The survey showed that during 1931-32 fourteen out of the fifty companies had made a loss, including Henry Page & Co, which had laid off sixteen of its 56 workers. For December 1932 the results were even worse and two-fifths of the malthouses in the United Kingdom were standing idle. The turning point was the budget of 1933, which outlined a 'gentleman's agreement' between the government, the brewers and farmers to which the malting industry was implicitly a partner. For this agreement Page Croft, as

Conservative MP for Christchurch, could claim some of the credit. The beer duty was reduced and in return the brewers were asked to reduce the price of a pint by a penny. Rather than impose higher duty on imported barley, the malting companies were encouraged to use as much home-grown barley as possible. In a speech to the Annual Banquet of the Institute of Brewing in 1939, Page Croft said

*Henry Page Croft (1881-1947)*
*1st Baron Croft*

Since 1931 the various Governments had passed into law no less than twenty different Acts directly aimed at giving security and prosperity to agriculture, and but for those Acts, certain branches of agriculture would not be today confronted with distress, but with positive ruin. Nature might yield prolifically in certain years, as was the case of barley in 1938, but the Government could not be blamed for that. As an impartial observer he would like to tell all those associated with agriculture that it was his belief that the brewing industry had during the last two years played the game under the gentleman's agreement and, on the whole, it had played more than the game.

Henry Page Croft stepped down as chairman of the family firm in 1940 when Winston Churchill made him Secretary of State for War in the House of Lords. He then became Baron Croft. Another mile stone was passed in 1932 when the ledgers of Henry Page & Co. showed that they had stopped dealing in Brown Malt.

# The Second World War and afterwards

The Second World War saw the repeat of the problems of 1914-18 – high taxation on beer, controls on the purchase of barley and malt, and staff shortages. The outbreak of war saw the requisition of many maltings for the storage of food. The arrival of large numbers of American and Empire troops in 1942 intensified the problem since they created a demand for more brewing malt which could not be met with the shortage of labour. In September 1943 the Brewers' Society said their main problem was the shortage of workers which resulted in many maltings remaining empty and brewers reducing output. Women were again employed in the malthouses, again on lower wages than the men they replaced. There was also bomb damage to maltings in some parts of the country – no malthouse was damaged in Ware although a house in New Road which had once belonged to the Dickinson family was destroyed by a high explosive bomb in September 1940.

One of the most welcome wartime changes became a serious problem afterwards. Combine harvesters were introduced from North America in the early years of the war and by 1944 it is estimated there were 2,500 in operation. Traditionally barley had been harvested, then stored and threshed when needed during the winter months, ensuring a steady supply to the maltsters. But the new combines created an immediate supply of grain which required both drying and storage by maltsters rather than farmers – a particularly acute problem in wet years. Government proposals to build communal grain driers were opposed by the maltsters because they did not account for different types of grain and different needs.

Henry Page & Co had built a grain drier and store in Star Street at the beginning of the war but it was destroyed by fire in 1946. Plans for a new barley-drying plant and silos were submitted to the local council in September 1948 and construction began the following year on a site next to the Victoria Maltings. The company was proud of the new plant and silo, which featured in a number of magazines including *The Brewers' Guardian* and *Food*. It was a six-storey brick

*A group of young women who worked in Ware maltings during the Second World War.*

building, with sixteen concrete grain bins, an electrical drier and mechanical handling connecting with the Victoria Maltings at roof level.

The first of the post-war improvements had been the establishment of a laboratory at the Henry Page offices at 85 High Street. The laboratory contained all the latest equipment for grinding and weighing barley and malt samples, measuring moisture and nitrogen content, as well as more sophisticated digestion, distillation and germination tests. One of those recruited was Jerome Murphy, later the chief chemist of Harrington Page & Co. Ltd.

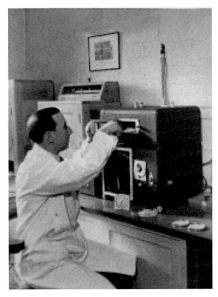

*Jerome Murphy at work*

The immediate post-war years were a difficult and drab period throughout the UK. There were shortages of all kinds, including power cuts, and rationing of food, petrol and other necessities was still in force. The Festival of Britain in 1951 with its displays of science, industry and the arts was an attempt by the Labour government to revive the nation's morale. But Ware had done something similar the year before. In March 1950, 'The Ware Exhibition (Trades and Hobbies)' was held in the Drill Hall, Amwell End, 'under the joint organization of the Rotary Club of Ware and the Ware Chamber of Trade'. The exhibition was open from 3 pm on Thursday 9 March until 8 pm on Saturday 11 March: price of admission was one shilling with sixpence for children. One of the most prominent stands – Stand No. 2 in the official programme – was the Ware Maltsters, featuring a large cut-away model of a malthouse (now in the Ware Museum), sacks of barley and malt bearing the names of the four malting companies represented and examples of modern malting equipment. All four malting companies – Gripper & Wightman, John Harrington, Henry Page & Co. and Henry Ward & Sons – had full-page advertisements in the programme and opposite that of Henry Page was an editorial about the stand and the history of the malt trade in Ware.

The maltsters' stand endeavours to present a composite picture of the malting trade as now conducted in Ware.

It illustrates the varieties of barley from which the maltster selects his raw material and shows models and photographs of the most modern plant now used for drying, sweating and storing the grain. Combine-harvesting of barley necessitates large drying and storing capacity, to receive the flood of grain from the farm before malting can commence.

The process of converting the barley to malt is demonstrated on a specially constructed model of a traditional malthouse, while the larger and more modern air-conditioned plant is illustrated by photographs. Some of the scientific apparatus used in the valuation of malt and barley is also shown.

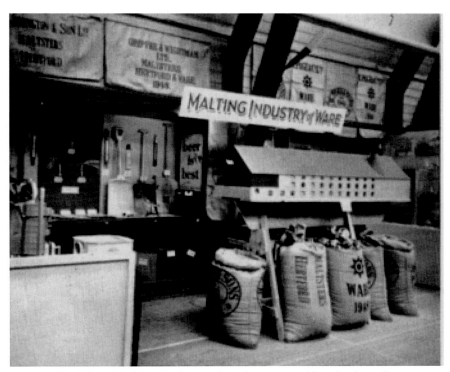

*The Ware Malting Industry Stand, arranged by the four firms
which in 1950 controlled all the maltings in the town*

The following article on the Malt Trade said that a hundred years before there had been 22 maltsters in the town. There had been amalgamations of many small malting businesses and modern road and rail transport had facilitated delivery of malt to London from more distant malting towns.

Despite many vicissitudes and the effect of heavy duty on beer, the Malting trade is still of outstanding importance and from this town malt is supplied, not merely to most of the large breweries in London but to many breweries great and small all over the country.

It was a brave attempt to capture the future for the Ware maltsters in a difficult and increasingly cut-throat business environment. The model of a traditional floor malting on Stand No. 2 showed how behind the times Ware firms were, even with the introduction of air-conditioning at the Victoria Maltings in

1939 to speed up germination of the barley. Already by 1950, there were more mechanised and labour-saving processes than the traditional floor malting, such as drums maltings and the 'Saladin Box', both of which made malting possible throughout the year and saved considerably on both space and labour.

The 1950s began three decades of business takeovers and mergers without precedent in British life and what was true of business as a whole was even more the case in malting and brewing. In 1946 the Maltsters' Association had 89 members but by 1975 there were only sixteen[6]. The norm was towards bigger and bigger companies, like Associated British Maltsters (ABM) and Pauls Malt, which between them accounted for half of the production of all sales maltsters by 1970. The process was for small company A to merge with small company B, then to merge with medium-sized company C which would be taken over by large company D. H.A. & D. Taylor of Sawbridgeworth – which owned maltings in Ware – merged with the Ipswich Malting Company in 1957 and the combined company was itself taken over by ABM the following year.

The Ware and Hertford maltsters could see the trend and in 1962-3 merged to form the firm of Harrington Page Ltd. The aim of the merger was to pool their resources so that the new company would have the capital and other wherewithal to construct a truly modern malthouse, a German Wanderhaufen or 'moving piece' malting. Work began in 1963 at Broadmeads in Ware, on a site next to the 1953 grain drier, but halfway through construction the company ran out of money. Ware folklore at one time provided various scenarios for this crisis, including a large insurance company reneging on a promise and a hurried but unsuccessful meeting at some motorway services. What is certain is that the builders encountered unexpected problems with a high water table while piling for the foundations – the site is in a part of Ware that used to flood annually. The outcome was that Harrington Page approached Pauls Malt of Ipswich, which bought them out for £575,000 and completed the project.

---

[6] Christine Clark, *The British Malting Industry since 1830* (Hambledon Press, 1998)., 191.

*The Victoria Maltings complex at Broadmeads in the 1970s. The* Wanderhaufen *malting was in the tall building with the white roof; to the right of it was the 1953 grain drier and to the right of that the 'old' Victoria Maltings, then redundant.*

# Pauls Malt at Broadmeads

The Wanderhaufen malting, manufactured by the German company Seeger, was finally installed at Broadmeads in 1965. Initially, it had a capacity of 74,000 quarters of barley or 13,000 tonnes but that was increased in 1977 to 17,000 and in the 1980s to 20,000 tonnes.

In exterior appearance, the new plant was quite unlike any malting in Ware. It consisted of two brick buildings, joined together and to the 1953 drier by conveyors. In these were 80 bins for storing grain – 40 for barley and 40 for malt. Outside were two silver-coloured barley silos as well as the 16 grain silos in the 1953 drier. The grain would stand for two to three weeks after drying so it could recover. It would go from the silo

*The mechanical screws or 'street worms' which constantly turned the germinating grain and moved it towards the kiln.*

to the holding bin and then into the steeps, of which there were twelve. The malting process began when two steeps were emptied on to one of the two 'streets' – meticulously clean, long passages on which the barley was constantly turned by mechanical screws, known as 'street worms'. The screws moved the grain closer to the kiln and after four days the germinating grain would be kilned and thus converted into malt. It was a plant which operated 24 hours a day, 365 days a year.

During the 1980s a mechanical refurbishment of the plant was undertaken, as well as computerisation of both the steeping and kilning. Controlling the steeping in this way was a major improvement, as the former manager Mr C.J. Claydon explained in a Pauls feature:

> During the steeping phase, if the temperature differential between the top and bottom probe exceeds 2°C, a signal is given to a pump which recirculates the water from the bottom to the top of the tank until the differential is within the set limits. This has proved to be invaluable particularly during the summer months when ambient temperatures can exceed 25°C.

Malting during the summer, especially with temperatures of that magnitude, is something that no Ware maltster could have achieved before. But computerisation went further. The use of Programme Logic Controllers and an efficient alarm system resulted in unmanned night running. If any fault occurred – or even a minor departure from the programme – then an alarm would ring at an office in Manchester and a manager in Ware would be telephoned. As Mr Claydon put it, "every operation that is performed on the site using the various control systems can be done from home". These changes greatly increased the productivity of the Ware site. The staff of twelve included, as well as the operatives, two men to clean the streets, an electrical engineer, a barley manager, a production manager and the maltster/manager with a secretary.

There were three operatives who actually made the malt, one working 6.00 am – 3.00 pm, the second 3.00 pm – midnight and the third on a day off. John Bevan, who was one of the last operatives to work at Pauls Malt in Broadmeads, said if there was a problem the shift maltster had to work until the problem was solved, even into the early hours. The main job was to keep the streets and tunnels clear and clean:

It was like cleaning a sewer in a gale and because there was so much water involved in making malt at Victoria Maltings it was a never ending job in keeping everything clean from growth etc. and at the other end of the procedures in drying and kilning. Dust, heat and noise were the problem; it was a very large area for one man to cover, and the main problem was that you could be working at one end of the maltings and if you got an alarm at the other end you had to drop everything and see to that problem.

The new street malting took over all the production of the 1907 Victoria Maltings, which was used for general storage for a number of years with small businesses, including a barge chandlery, occupying the ground floor next to the Cut. In the 1980s the old building was sold to a developer and burned down one evening in September 1988.

**END OF AN ERA**

**Ware's malt link severed**

HUNDREDS of years of malt making for the brewing industry have come to an end in Ware.

The last remaining working malt plant in the town is closing at the end of the week.

Pauls Malt at Victoria Maltings in Broadmeads makes 20,000 tonnes annually but says company managing director David Ringrose: "There is a general downturn in beer consumption, and also whisky, and the world recession is having its effect."

Stunned workers were taking stock of the news last week. "It's the end of an era," said the site's general manager Tim Hyland. "Ware at one point was the most important malting town in the UK."

And saddened Ware Society's David Perman added: "It will be the first time in about 650 years that malt has not been made in Ware. The town's fortunes were based on malt — certainly since the Elizabethan period. There were well over 100 kilns — about 50-60 maltings."

Ware malt even had its own price at one time on the London markets and brown malt, the basis of a stout

● TIM Hyland at the doomed plant

*How the* Hertfordshire Mercury *announced the closure of the Pauls Malt Victoria Maltings.*

## End of an Era

On 6 January 1994, Pauls Malt announced that they were closing their Ware operation. The local newspaper reported the managing director David Ringrose as saying: "There is a general downturn in beer consumption, and also whisky, and the world recession is having its effect."

Four days later I interviewed the manager, Tim Hyland (photographed in the *Mercury* outside the plant at Broadmeads) and he enlarged on the reasons for the closure. He said that the biggest single factor was that world consumption of beer had dropped dramatically, during the current world recession, and the malt requirement was heavily reduced. In addition, many maltsters throughout the world were expanding their capacity and building new plants without closing the old plants. Competition from the French in particular, selling their malt to brewers at "ridiculously low prices", had hammered prices. The Ware site was being closed because it was a small site but with "real-estate value". But it had had an excellent record for productivity.

> That's the ironic thing really. The site at Ware runs with twelve people, including myself, which is probably the lowest-manned malting unit in the whole of the UK. We are extremely efficient and our costs even have reflected that as well. It's also a very attractive site: internally the paintwork and the general appearance of the plant is very appealing by malting standards. So it is ironic that this particular site is closing but, unfortunately, because of its location and its size – it is actually the smallest malting unit that we have in the group – and the fact that we could regain some capital from selling it, has obviously been the downfall of us really.

The malt production at Ware was transferred to Paul's plant at Wallingford, which itself closed in 1998. In that year Pauls Malt was sold to the Anglo-Swiss commodity trading and mining company Glencore but still maintained its malting operations in Bury St. Edmunds, Knapton in Yorkshire and two sites in Scotland, at Glenesk and Buckie. Since 2010, however, Pauls has been part of the Belgian conglomerate, Boortmalt NV, which claims to be the fifth largest producer of malt in the world and the second in Europe.

But that was not quite the end of the malting industry in Ware . . . . .

*The maltmaker statue by the Oxfordshire sculptor, Jill Tweed,
unveiled on 4 November 1999 to mark the Millennium
and the end of 600 years of malt-making in Ware.*

*The unveiling was done by Hugo Page Croft, the great great
grandson of Henry Page and himself a former maltster at the
Moray-Firth Maltings in Scotland.*

# The Ware Maltmaker

The idea of commemorating the malting industry was discussed by the author with Guy Horlock, chairman of the Stanstead Abbotts maltsters, French and Jupp Ltd. The firm is the last working maltster in Hertfordshire, specialising in the production of top-quality coloured malts for the food and drinks industry. Guy approached the managing director, David Jupp, who got the agreement of his Board to commission drawings for a sculpture. Hugo Page Croft then joined the committee.

The sculptor chosen was Jill Tweed from Bampton, Oxon, who had worked on a similar industrial project of a bargeman at Sittingbourne in Kent. Jill was sent drawings of Ware maltmakers, including the one below, and produced a maquette of a maltmaker and his cat (all maltings had a cat). This was approved and Jill was commissioned to make the final sculpture in clay, which was cast in bronze at a foundry in High Wycombe. Funding for the project was provided by French and Jupp Ltd., and also by the charitable fund of Scottish and Newcastle Brewery of which Hugo Page Croft was a former director. The unveiling on 4 November 1999 in the Memorial Garden in the High Street was done before a large crowd of well-wishers, including many former Ware maltmakers.

# Malting dynasties

Family relationships played an important role in the history of Ware's malting industry. The right marriage at the right time was often the key to future success and prosperity – as will be seen from the following:.

## ADAMS

Members of the Adams family had been engaged in malting in Ware since the early 1700s. Pigot's Directory for 1823-24 included Samuel Adams, maltster and malt factor with offices in Water Row (the south side of the High Street). He was the factor for Reid, Meux brewery and his base was the Cannon Maltings in Baldock Street. During the 1830s he built himself a house next to the malting and called it Cannons. Pigot's directories also listed Adams as a banker. In 1813 Samuel and his brother Thomas Adams, both described as maltsters, bargeowners and coal merchants, set up the Ware Bank in Water Row and a year later acquired the Hertford and Ware Bank (quite distinct from the Ware Bank of Cass and Chuck). The *Bankers Magazine* for 1846 reported that the bank had fixed capital of £23,635 and gave the directors as Samuel Adams of Ware, maltster, and his nephew Samuel Adams jnr. of Ware, also a maltster. Samuel Adams died in 1850 and was succeeded at the bank by his nephew. All went well until 22 July 1856 when the Hertford branch did not open, followed by the Ware branch failing to open. Then one of the bank's depositors served a Petition in Bankruptcy. Over the next year, the courts seized all of Samuel Adams's properties, malt, stocks, furniture and a barge called the 'Mary Ann'. The sale of those assets realised almost £12,000 which went to public creditors like the Collector of Taxes while other depositors received nothing. Henry Page lost his first fortune and the family legend was that Samuel Adams had absconded to Australia, clutching a bag of gold. But the Court of Bankruptcy found that he had made large and unwise loans to a swindler, named Captain Johnson. Page was not the only maltster to suffer. Another, William Cater, was declared bankrupt when he could not pay £9,800 he owed in excise duty.

*The memorial in St. Mary's to John (left) and George Cass (right) and their respective children.*

## CASS

The Cass family were well established in Ware in 1632 when the first of a succession of family members named 'Aaron Casse' was born to Robert Casse and his wife Mary. In 1713, Aaron Cass described as an innholder was one of the 'feoffees of the town rents' – i.e. a trustee of what later became Ware Charities. His son, Aaron Cass the younger, was a maltster and an overseer of the poor – he was concerned with others in building a poor workhouse in Crib Street. The Cass family were related to both the Dickinson and Docwra families. The most successful member of the family was George Cass (1753-1826) who went from maltster to 'gentleman' and in the 1820s became a director of the Ware Bank, alongside his son John and son-in-law Edward Chuck, both maltsters – a pound note signed by the three of them is in the Ware Museum collection. Both George and John Cass have memorials in St. Mary's where they are described as 'malt factors'. John had twelve children by his wife, Sophia, including quadruplets – two boys and two girls – born in 1826. One of these was Charles Cass who followed the family tradition as a maltster and also built Presdales Mansion in Hoe Lane (later occupied by the Sandemann and McMullen families, both in the drinks business). The Cass malthouses were in Baldock Street, the High Street and Hoe Lane.

## CHUCK

The Chuck family came into the malting business in the eighteenth century, but had other strings to their bows. John Chuck (1756-1806) was described as a 'maltster' in 1804 but in his will he was said to be a 'victualler' i.e. a grocer. He was married to Ann Want and they had six children. The oldest, Susanna, married Lieut. Thomas Collins, who had been promoted from the ranks in the Dragoon Guards – they lived in New Road and had five children, including Captain Thomas Chuck Collins, who was killed in Afghanistan, and Ann Elizabeth, who married the maltster Henry Page. Two of John and Ann's other children became maltsters – Edward (1783-1852) and Joseph (1786-1859).

Edward was married to Elizabeth Cass and initially went into business with her brother John as a plumber and glazier: later they were both directors of the Ware Bank with Edward's father-in-law, George Cass. Edward lived at 87 High Street and his initials and the date 1827 exist on the lead rainwater heads: he may well have been responsible for enlarging the eighteenth-century house and adding the portico and classical columns. Edward worked the maltings originally built by Thomas Docwra in the yard to the rear; he was also a malt factor for Courage and Whitbread breweries and on friendly terms with both families, as well as the family of Thomas William Coke, Earl of Leicester, at Holkham Hall in Norfolk. Edward also farmed at Noah's Ark Farm near Fanhams Hall. It was while driving a chaise to his

*Edward Chuck's grand tomb, erected by his widow
in the old churchyard in Church Street.*

farm in 1852 that he was involved in a collision with a cart in High Oak Lane. Edward's right knee was smashed and, although he received the best medical attention, he died two days later. His funeral was a grand affair, attended by family, Ware maltsters and one Whitbread and three Courage brothers. Later his widow had an elaborate tomb erected in the old burial ground in Church Street. She also used their fortune to found the Chuck Memorial School on Musley Hill (later a grammar school, infants' school and now a nursery).

There seems to have been a coldness if not a feud between Susanna and Edward, on the one side, and their brother Joseph. He too was a maltster but, although he was mentioned in Edward's will, he did not inherit the maltings behind 87 High Street. Instead they went to Susanna's son-in-law, Henry Page. Joseph and his son Silas were trustees of the Ware Charities which owned the town's existing Grammar School and were opposed to the setting up of the Chuck Memorial School. There were religious differences also. Susanna and Edward were staunch supporters of St. Mary's Parish Church, where Edward installed the East Window in memory of their parents, but Joseph was a Nonconformist. When a new Congregational church and Sunday School were being planned, Joseph offered to pay half the cost of the church and the whole cost of the school. Joseph was in the malting business with his son, Silas, who was also a builder and surveyor: their maltings were in the High Street and Dead Lane (Church Street).

## COBHAM

The Cobhams were an important family in nineteenth-century Ware. Nathaniel Cobham was listed as an attorney in Pigot's Directory for 1832 – in 1882 either he or his son was a solicitor, clerk to the magistrates and clerk to the local board of health with an office in Baldock Street. William Cobham was a malt factor living in Water Row (High Street) in the 1823 directory and again in 1839, but in 1850 he was declared bankrupt with all his 'real and personal estate' being granted in trust to Isaac Kimpton Waller, Thomas Heaver and Caleb Hitch the younger to pay his creditors. His son, William Cobham jnr, had a malting company in Amwell End and lived at The Grange, a large house at the corner of London Road and Hoe Lane – demolished for road widening in 1972. William jnr was in partnership with Thomas Cobham as barge owners, but the partnership was dissolved in 1842. Another branch of the family was centred on John Cobham who in 1839 was listed as John Cobham & Son, maltster and malt factor, in the High Street. He and his wife Susan had four children, the oldest of whom, Susan Matilda Cobham, married Silas Chuck, the son of Joseph Chuck.

## COWELL

John Cowell was a maltster and malt factor in the High Street in 1826, and later in Crib Street. He was married to Emma, the oldest child of the maltster Joseph Chuck and died in 1849. His son, John Cowell Jnr. was a maltster and also an artist. An album of his sketches of coastal scenes and ships is in the Yale Center for British Art in New Haven, Connecticut, and is dedicated to his father and brother George. John Cowell was still in business in Crib Street in the Kelly's Directory for 1899 but there is no sign of him in the twentieth century.

## DICKINSON

The Dickinson family combined success in the Ware malting industry with running one of London's major breweries. They arrived in the town in the reign of Elizabeth I and after the Restoration in 1660 there were three Dickinson brothers engaged in the malting business. Rivers Dickinson in 1700 owned a house

*The large brick house in East Street where the maltster*
*Joseph Dickinson lived and*
*(below) a rainwater head with the date 1709 and his initials JD.*

and malting at 55 High Street – between the Bull's Head and the King's Head inns. Richard Dickinson was involved in transporting malt to London and in 1694 took a lead in seeking the removal of further obstacles to navigation on the Lea. Joseph Dickinson lived in a splendid brick house in Land Row (East Street) and had maltings directly to the north and east. The location of Mr. Dickinson's house and malthouse is shown on a 1685 map of the Place House school for the children of Christ's Hospital. The school's records show that "the cinders from Mr. Dickinson's maltings next door blew in through the Place House windows, so that the schoolmaster asked for window shutters".

The Dickinsons became London brewers in spite of themselves. In 1690, Rivers Dickinson was owed nearly £1,000 for malt by a Captain Boreham, a "considerable brewer in Whitechapel", and to get his money he was forced to manage the brewhouse himself. He failed and lost a further £1,000 – "from want of skill in the affairs of brewing and the failing of the victuallers he dealt with, who run away". Yet the business survived and in 1739 a younger member of the family, Joseph (son of Joseph Dickinson of East Street), was bound apprentice to him and later set himself up at the Cannon Brewery in St. John Street, Clerkenwell. For the next hundred years or so, different members of the family continued brewing in London – in Clerkenwell and in Red Lion Street, Holborn. In Ware, they carried on malting, intermarried with other malting families – Docwra and Cass – acquired more malthouses in Water Row, Crib Street and Amwell End, where one of the yards demolished to make way for the Drill Hall in 1899 was called Dickinson's Yard. They also advanced up the social scale. In 1808 John Baron Dickinson – a wealthy brewer, maltster, maltfactor and barge owner and a grandson of Joseph Dickinson of East Street – went into partnership with John and Thomas Green to found the first of Ware's banks. Their customers included all the well-known maltsters and other public figures in Ware. They continued in business until 1 October 1813 when the partnership was dissolved 'by mutual consent'.

John Baron Dickinson died in 1829 and the memorial to him is one of many to the family in St. Mary's Church, despite the Dickinsons having been originally non-Anglican Independents. One of the most fulsome – in the floor of the North Transept – is to Mary, wife of Richard Dickinson ...

whose virtue and sincere behaviour
both in a single and a married state
were equalled by few, exceeded by none ...

Beside the memorial to John Baron Dickinson – see opposite page – is another which indicates that the male line of the family would shortly be dying out. It is to William Dickinson, a student at Clare Hall, Cambridge, who died aged 23, and was erected in

*Two of the memorials to the Dickinson family*
*in the South Aisle of St. Mary's Church.*

1828 by John Baron, his wife and sister ..

> who had fondly viewed him as the Prop
> of their fast-declining Years, but the
> merciful God, who beheld, approved,
> and took him to himself, will over their
> wounded hearts, pour the soothing
> balm of reflecting on the bliss he now
> enjoys, and the cheering hope, that
> they, ere long, shall partake therein.

Accordingly, with the death of John Baron and his cousin Jonathan, the Dickinson property in East Street was sold along with the malting yard and garden behind. The timber-framed malthouses were either demolished or cut back. A few years later, New Road was constructed with model terraced houses for malting workers. Mrs Martha Dickinson and her sister, Ann, went to live in a large house in New Road on what is now misspelt as 'Dickenson Way' – leading to Tesco's carpark.

*The two-storey 'Dutch summerhouse' behind No. 63 High Street was probably built by John Docwra during the reign of William III ('Dutch William') – a dated brick bears the date 1697 and the intitials of his wife, Mary Docwra née Dickinson.*

## DOCWRA

The Docwras came to Ware in the seventeenth century from Bassingbourn in Cambridgeshire and were originally Quakers. They grew wealthy in the malting industry. In his will Thomas Docwra (1639-1695) left his eldest son John his dwelling house at 63 High Street, a considerable number of meadows and cowleases and also "the use and proffitt of the five new Maltshopps which I lately built being in the Yard belonging to the Crowne Inn in Ware". The malt-shops were to go to the youngest son, Thomas, when he reached twenty-one; a middle son, Joseph, got all the family land in Little Amwell, south of Ware Bridge, and two daughters, Mary and Sarah, received £600 each. The oldest son, John (1677-1741) married Mary Dickinson of the neighbouring malting family – the sister of Rivers, Richard and Joseph. When John Docwra (described as a 'malster') died in 1741, he was reckoned to be worth £4,400 and left £1,400 to his sons John and Thomas and his daughter Mary. When John's widow Mary died in 1747 she left bequests to her nephews and nieces of the Cass, Dickinson, Grindall, Kettle and Mansell families – all maltsters. George Docwra (a great grandson) sold

No. 63 High Street to Nathaniel Page in 1848. The former Crown Inn and its malt-shops had passed to Edward Chuck earlier.

## GRIPPER

The Gripper family had interests in both Hertford and Ware and seem to have been Quakers at one time. In 1744 Thomas Gripper of Ware, maltster, bought from Rivers Dickinson a house 'with a new brick front' at the western end of Kibes Lane where it joined Back Street (East Street) together with a malthouse with kiln and two barns and three stables. This is a fascinating document for it relates to the time before New Road was constructed and mentions 'a short way or street, leading to the Great Road or Highway to the south' – i.e. the High Street. In 1747, Thomas's son by his wife Mary Hampson, daughter of Wayte Hampson of Ware, malt factor, was bound apprentice to another maltster, Thomas Fage. Most of the later references are to Grippers in Hertford, where they were active in local politics as Liberals: Thomas Gripper was Mayor of Hertford first in 1830. They were also barge owners and dealt in corn, coal and iron rods. The malting firm of Gripper & Wightman was active before the First World War and was honoured for supporting the Army in France – their maltings were mainly in Star Street.

## HANBURY

Sampson Hanbury (1769-1835) was not a maltster but he had an enormous influence on Ware malting. He purchased Truman's brewery in Shoreditch in 1788 and went on to run it for 46 years. He was married to the granddaughter of David Barclay of Youngsbury, another Quaker brewer, and – because of his wife's association with the area – took a lease on Poles, just north of Ware, in 1800 and purchased it in 1820. Hanbury took a great interest in the supply of malt and appointed three factors for Truman's – William Adams for Ware, John Taylor for Bishop's Stortford and John Kemp for Essex and the rest of East Anglia. In 1808 Hanbury took into partnership his nephew, Thomas Fowell Buxton, who was an MP and campaigner against the slave trade – his son, another Thomas Fowell Buxton, purchased the Easneye estate at Stanstead Abbots.

## HANKIN

The Hankin family was based in Ware and Stanstead Abbots and clearly very wealthy. When the London brewer Henry Thrale – a friend of Dr Samuel Johnson – embarked upon the mad scheme of trying to brew beer without malt and in 1772 amassed debts of £130,000, his wife Hester had to raise money from her friends – including Mrs Hankin, the mother of a Ware maltfactor, who lent her £6,000. It is reported that at the time Thrale & Co. owed Hankin £6,400 for malt. Hankin specialised in brown malt and sold it widely. The records of Cobbs' brewery in Margate show that from at least 1782 until 1806 they were getting their malt from Hankin & Son of Ware.

## HITCH

In 1742 the Hitch family were bricklayers who owned a property in Middle Row near the Vine Inn – 'The Lodge' is now on the site. In 1797 this was conveyed to Miss Sarah Hitch, Miss Ann Hitch and Mr Caleb Hitch – the first of four Calebs in the family. His son Caleb Hitch the Younger (1785-1851) added malting and brickmaking to the family's trades. In 1828 he patented 'a wall built of bricks with cavities in them', in other words his patent bricks, and with them constructed a number of buildings, including the Rose and Crown pub in Watton Road and a large malting in Park Road – now part of the Asda supermarket. Caleb III carried on his father's trade of brickmaking and building (in 1862 he built the Star Brewery in Watton Road) but his main business was malting. He owned maltings behind Baldock Street and in Star Street. Other members of the Hitch family were builders and bargemakers at the Dockyard in Star Street. Caleb Hitch & Son, maltsters, ceased trading in 1939. The last member of the family engaged in malting was Ernest Hollingsworth Hitch (1861-1941) who lived at 27 Baldock Street and was the father of the Ware historian Edith Hunt.

## KIMPTON

Pigot's Directory for 1839 under the heading 'maltsters' lists Thomas Kimpton in Star Street and Isaac Kimpton Waller in

High Street. They are examples of the tangled relationships in the Ware malting industry. Isaac (1792-1864) was the son of Thomas Waller, described as a corn-chandler, and Elizabeth Kimpton – her father was William Kimpton (probably the brother of Thomas Kimpton) who farmed at Fanhams Hall. In 1815 William bought another farm, at Mackhouse on the back road to Babb's Green, and took out a mortgage from the maltster Edward Chuck, who owned the nearby Noah's Ark Farm. Isaac was an important enough person in the malting industry to act as a trustee along with Thomas Heaver and Caleb Hitch in the bankruptcy case of the malt factor, William Cobham, in 1850.

## PAGE

Henry Page (1812-1894) was the most successful – and certainly the richest – maltster in Ware, but he started out in a modest manner. Like his father and grandfather he was a baker – the Census for 1841 shows him aged 29 as a baker in Upper Land Row (West Street). The bakery was in Churchgate House, later known as Jaggs & Edwards and now Jacoby's restaurant. He married Anne Elizabeth Collins and their only child, also named Anne Elizabeth, was born in 1843. In the 1851 Census, Henry was described as a maltster employing 30 men. Two or three years later, Henry and Anne moved into 87 High Street which her mother had inherited in the will of Edward Chuck. With the house went the maltings and also the neighbouring house, 85 High Street, formerly the home of Dr. McNab and then the offices of Henry Page & Co. By all accounts Henry Page was an enterprising and resourceful businessman. His grandson, Henry Page Croft, told the story of Henry travelling to London with a younger colleague who suggested putting their travelling rugs in the Left Luggage at Liverpool Street; 'No, no,' said Henry Page, the pawn shop round the corner was cheaper. But it was not all plain sailing. Henry Page claimed to have lost one fortune when the Ware Bank under Samuel Adams jnr collapsed in 1856. Nevertheless, when Henry Page died in 1894 in his 82nd year he left an estate worth £1,087,000 – worth more than £100m in today's money. This fortune was inherited by his only child, Anne Elizabeth, who was married to Richard Benyon

*Richard Benyon Croft (1843-1912) in his naval uniform,*
*and Anne Elizabeth née Page (1843-1921)*
*– a photograph taken by her keen photographer husband.*

Croft, a retired naval officer. Mrs Croft used part of her inheritance to purchase the Priory for the town of Ware and part to refurbish Fanhams Hall as a stately home. In a letter to Gladstone in 1880, Henry Page had said he controlled 40 maltings in Ware and Hertford. But the number grew and by 1895 the company was producing over 60,000 quarters of malt a season, three-quarters of which went to one customer, the brewery Combe & Co.

After Henry Page's death, the malting company remained in family hands, under Richard Benyon Croft, then his two sons Richard Page Croft and Henry Page Croft, and finally Richard's son, another Richard. Henry Page Croft had been an MP since 1910, as well as serving in the First World War where he was promoted to Brigadier. In 1940 Winston Churchill made him Secretary of State for War in the House of Lords, as Baron Croft. He consequently resigned as a director of Henry Page & Co.

The last member of the family engaged in the malting industry was Hugo Page Croft (born 1944), a co-founder of the Moray Firth Malting Company, supplying whisky distillers, and later a director of Scottish and Newcastle Brewery Co. Ltd. Hugo is a great, great grandson of Henry Page.

## SCOTT

In 1740, Samuel Scott moved from Southwark, where he had owned a tannery, to a house in Amwell End known as The Peacock. – now Amwell House. The move was made to set up the family in the malting business, including his two sons, Samuel jnr (1719-88) and John (1731-83). They were Quakers and probably had friends or relatives among the Quaker maltsters of Ware and Hertford. Samuel jnr later became a Quaker preacher in Hertford, while John remained in Ware enlarging the house and creating a large garden with summerhouses and a grotto. John was active in local affairs as an overseer of the poor and member of three turnpike trusts. He was also a poet. Their malthouses were probably in London Road and Hoe Lane.

## SWORDER

John Sworder (1797-1878) came from a farming family and was born in Standon. Around 1820 he started in the Ware malting industry with a dwelling and office in Water Row. His older brother Robert, who was still farming, owned a malt kiln in Mill Lane (Priory Street). Pigot's Directory for 1839 shows John as a maltster and malt factor in the High Street joined nearby by Charles Sworder, perhaps another brother. Other members of the family were established in Hertford as solicitors and a town clerk – and later as auctioneers and estate agents.

## TAYLOR

John Taylor was the maltfactor in Ware for the brewer Sampson Hanbury, who lived at Poles north of the town. He was the son of Samuel Taylor, a barge-owner and maltster who had bought a small property beside Ware Bridge in 1786, about the same time John had moved to Stortford with the opening up of the Stort Navigation. These Taylors were ancestors of the prominent Sawbridgeworth firm of maltsters, H.A.& D. Taylor Ltd. The main point here is that John Taylor's relationship with Sampson Hanbury went beyond business affairs. They were close personal friends and Taylor would visit Hanbury's in-laws, the Gurney family, whenever he visited Norfolk.

*The Home Yard of Henry Ward and Son behind 63 High Street and (below) initials of some of the directors on the kiln built in 1885.*

# WARD

In 1850 Henry Ward started a malting business with William Hudson, who also farmed at Noah's Ark Farm – where he succeeded Edward Chuck. In 1859 they owned four maltings, two in Brewster's Yard, one in the yard behind 63 High Street where Mr Hudson lived, and one at Bridgefoot. Hudson died in 1868, after which Henry Ward continued the business alone. The business grew rapidly and in 1896 the company owned 18 maltings, some of which were in Hertford and Bishop's Stortford. Ward's first wife was Hudson's daughter Annie, whose mother was a relative of Henry Page, a connection which brought money to the marriage. There were ten children from that marriage. After Annie's death in 1884 Henry Ward married Frances Emily Price. Ward was joined in the business by his sons, Harry, William and Charles – the first Harry was killed in the South African war. Henry Ward died after an accident in 1908, and William and Charles continued the business in the name of Henry Ward & Sons. In 1898 the Hope Maltings were purchased and the total number of maltings had increased to 24. Most of the malting kilns were reconstructed with air shafts to ensure better drying of the malt, and the old tiles used for kiln floors were replaced by wedge-wire floors.

Modernisation and the installation of machinery for screening and conveying the barley took place between the two world wars. In 1929 – for the first time in England – a forced draught kiln with a pressure chamber known as a 'Winckler' was erected at the top of the Star Street Maltings. Yet the maltings behind 63 High Street formed the 'Home Yard' of Henry Ward & Sons and here the company built a four-storey brick kiln in 1885. The business became a private limited company in 1935 with registered capital of £55,000. In the programme of the 1950 Ware Exhibition, Henry Ward & Sons said that several of the employees, both staff and maltmakers, had worked for the firm for over 30 years.

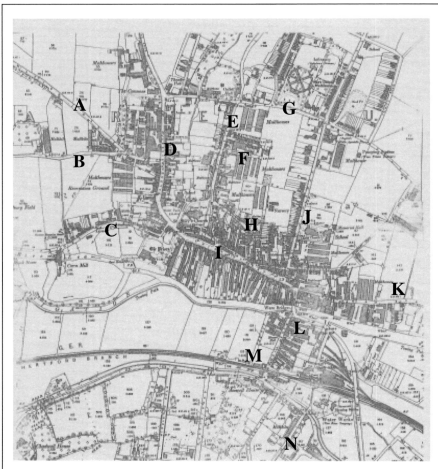

The proliferation of maltings, as shown on the Ordnance Survey map of Ware in 1896. The key to the roads in which most of the malt kilns were located is as follows:

A  Watton Road      B  Park Road        C  Priory Street
D  Baldock Street    E  Crib Street       F  Francis Road
G  Collett Road/The Bourne              H  Church Street
I  High Street       J  New Road         K  Star Street
L  Amwell End       M  Broadmeads       N  Hoe Lane

*Baldock Street on a postcard of about 1910. The buildings on the left are still there, but the Hope Maltings on the right was demolished for road widening when the Inner Relief Road was being planned. The fire station and a grass verge are there now – see description on the next page.*

## Maltings – past and present

The following pages feature former maltings which have been refurbished for other uses and the main malthouses which have disappeared – often leaving just a name behind.

The size of maltings was measured in terms of their steeping capacity, in other words the amount of grain which could be steeped in one batch. If the cistern could accommodate 30 quarters of barley then it was said to be a 30-quarter malthouse. Until the middle of the nineteenth century most malthouses had a capacity of less than 50 quarters. The quarter was the standard measure – it was equivalent to 8 bushels and was a measure of capacity rather than weight: a quarter of barley weighed 384lb (174 kg) and a quarter of malted barley – malt – weighed 272lb (123kg).

## Amwell End

A large malthouse behind 9 and 11 Amwell End is shown on nineteenth-century maps and also on the Britain from Above website – *www.britainfromabove.org.uk* – in an Aerofilms photo of 1929. It was later incorporated in the Frenlite mill of J.W. French & Co. and now forms part of the residential Millacres development.

The Maltings Surgery at 15 Amwell End was formerly the Cherry Tree public house, which was built in the 19th century but with remnants of 17th century timber framing. The pub had its own malting but this was demolished when the Drill Hall was built in 1899.

## Baldock Street

No 27 Baldock Street, an imposing eighteenth-century building in red brick, belonged to Ernest Hollingsworth Hitch, who was a maltster and chairman of the Ware Urban District Council in 1908. In this house his daughter, the Ware historian Edith Hunt was born in 1888. Behind the house was E.H. Hitch's malting yard, consisting of three two-storey malthouses, brick with timber ends. After malting ceased, the yard was known as 'Brewery Yard' and became a builders' yard associated with Crook Brothers with an entry from Watton Road. Two of the original malthouses still exist – one with the cowl of the malt kiln intact and the other minus the cowl – they can be seen from the Buryfield Recreation Ground.. At the time of writing, Crook Brothers no longer use the yard and it seems likely to become a development site.

Farther up Baldock Street were the Hope Maltings demolished in 1969 to make way for the Inner Relief Road, which in fact was never constructed although the wide roundabout was. At this point, Baldock Street used to proceed north in a straight line from the Old Bull's Head pub. One part of the Hope Maltings was right on the road, extending almost to opposite the Bourne.

*The Cannons Maltings, parts of which dated from 1612,*
*demolished in the sixties to make way for housing.*

An entrance from Baldock Street gave on to a wide yard, with another malting directly opposite and a third malting, running north and parallel to the one on the road. At the Watton Road end of the maltings was Hope House, for the maltster or his foreman, with a mulberry tree in the garden – the mulberry tree still exists now in the middle of the Watton Road roundabout. The Hope Maltings were built in the 1830s with three malting floors and cast-iron columns supporting the upper floors. At the time of the Malt Tax the three malthouses were identified as Nos. 5, 11 and 12 with capacitgies of 30 qrs, 60qrs and 40 qrs. respectively. An early owner was Edward Chuck who also occupied Hope House; later came James Hudson and then his relative by marriage, Henry Ward until 1963. The last owners before demolition were Harrington Page Ltd. Part of Baldock Street and the Ware Fire Station now occupy the site.

Immediately north of the Hope Maltings was a house known as Cannons, which became the residence of Samuel Adams, maltster and banker. At one time there was debate about the origin of the name 'Cannons' which also existed until recently in the Cannon Tavern in the Bourne – it was probably the name of an eighteenth-century owner. The house later became a hotel, known at first as the Cannons Hotel and then as the Roebuck before its demolition in 2016 to make way for a care home.

North of the house was the Cannons Malting – a vast range of malthouses, including one set back from the road behind a garden and another directly abutting the Wadesmill Road. Both of these were built in the early nineteenth century and had tie plates by Charles Well and J. Copsey. Between them was a much older building dating from the seventeenth century (a dated brick said: 'I.C. 1622') with a gateway and a three-light window with mullions of moulded brick. Behind these buildings were five other maltings, built at a lower level from the Wadesmill Road. The whole range was owned by Samuel Adams, then by Berkeley Brackenbury & Co, then by Henry Page & Co. Malting ceased in 1957 after which the maltings were used as a store for television sets by Thorn Electrical Industries. In the late 1960s Ware Urban District Council bought the site by compulsory purchase, demolished all the malthouses and built the Lower Bourne Gardens residential area.

**The Bourne**

There were two malthouse on the north side of The Bourne – formerly known as 'Bourne Hill'. The larger one incorporated Nos. 27-29 The Bourne and parts of it survive in a house which looks like a barn. It was at one time owned by Thomas Adams and was identified as Malting No. 23. The other malting ran along the side of the Upper Bourne stream in what is now Orchard Close.

**Bridgefoot**

There were maltings on both sides of Bridgefoot. Those on the east side were associated with The Barge Inn, demolished in about 1926 when the electricity company built North Met House (now the Waterside pub). On the west side of the bridge was a group of maltings with attractive cowls, beautifully captured in a watercolour by May Hammond and used as the frontispiece for Edith Hunt's *History of Ware* – see opposite page. These malt kilns included one behind the old Saracen's Head Inn and came down to the riverside, but did not have any wharfing for

*Maltings at Bridgefoot and behind the old Saracen's Head Inn –*
*from a watercolour by May Hammond, which formed the frontispiece of*
The History of Ware *by Edith Hunt (1946). Note the 'mortarboard' kiln*
*cowl on the right and the more modern revolving cowl on the left.*

loading barges. Some were demolished in 1939. The remainder
were demolished in the 1950s when the road from the bridge
was realigned to do away with the right-angle turn into the High
Street. The old Saracen's Head Inn was demolished in 1957.

*Broadmeads in 1987, showing – right to left – the 'old' Victoria Maltings built in 1907, the grain drier of 1953 and the two buildings completed in 1965 by Pauls Malt for the Wanderhaufen malting.*

### Broadmeads

Broadmeads was the site of Ware's biggest malthouse, the Victoria Maltings, built by Henry Page & Co. in 1907. In its day it was one of the most modern maltings in Britain, with five malting floors each with a steep of 40 qrs. capacity which were filled mechanically from a large barley store near the river. The kilns were similarly filled and discharged mechanically through ports in the wire floors. In 1938 the Victoria Maltings was one of the first to have air-conditioning installed. In 1953, a tall grain silo and drying plant was built next to the Victoria Maltings to replace a drier in Star Street which burned down in 1947. The Victoria Maltings was taken out of production in the 1960s and used for storage; it was later sold to a property developer and burned down one evening in September 1988.

In 1962 Henry Page & Co. merged with Henry Ward & Co. and the Hertford firms of John Harrington and Son and Gripper and

Wightman to form Harrington Page Ltd. This new company began to build an ultra-modern malthouse in 1964 using the German technology of Seeger to instal a 'Wanderhaufen street malting'. This was a fully automated plant which could operate 24 hours a day, 365 days a year, with minimal human contact. However, the building proved more costly than estimated and in 1965 Harrington Page was taken over by Pauls and Sandars of Ipswich and Gainsborough – later Pauls Malt. The plant was expanded in the 1980s and completely computerised. But in 1994, in the face of intense international competition, Pauls closed their Broadmeads malting – bringing to an end all maltmaking in Ware after 600 years. All the malting buildings were later demolished: a brick-built block and warehouse for Farécla Products Ltd were built on the sites of the 1907 Victoria Maltings and corn drier, and the Fusion Court flats on the sites of the Pauls Malt plant and silos.

## Church Street

On the 1851 Ordnance Survey map (in French Horn Lane as it was then named) maltings are shown on four sides of what is now Sucklings Yard. Next to that was a gate giving access to a yard in which there were two long maltings of brick with timber ends. These were known as the Alma Maltings and were built by Caleb Hitch in 1855, as indicated on a dated brick. But another dated brick in the garden wall of the cottage near the entrance said T.G. 1756. They were owned by Henry Page & Co. and identified as maltings Nos. 7 & 8. Malting ceased there in 1948 and the yard is now part of the Tesco carpark.

On the south side of Church Street, there was a malting behind the Lion and Wheatsheaf pub, which later became part of Ware Garage and is now incorporated in the Tesco supermarket. Farther to the west was a pair of maltings with dormer windows in their tiled roofs. They were owned at one time by Edward Chuck and later became part of the Stadium engineering works. The site is now part of Tudor Square in West Street and Tudor Walk in Church Street.

## Crib Street

Crib Street was crowded with maltings – as can be seen by the forest of malt cowls in the photograph taken from the terrace in front of Western House (see page 6).

The 1851 Ordnance Survey map shows maltings on the east side behind the cottages north of what is now the Albion; also a largish malting behind the Red Cow pub. Also five parallel maltings running north-south off Francis Road as well as the Omega maltings.

The maps of 1851 and 1880 show three malthouses on the corner of what is now Collett Road but then formed part of The Bourne. They were set back from the road in the same way that the present flats are. They were known as Nos. 16, 21 and 22 – No 22 was the largest of the three with a double kiln and was also known as the 'Great Western Group'. All three were demolished in the 1960s when two blocks of flats, known as 'The Maltings', were built on the footprints of Nos. 16 and 22.

On the west side of Crib Street was a malting adjoining the road, next to what is now no. 25, the Smoke House. Part of this malting may still exist in Nos. 29-33 Crib Street. In the early part of the 19th century it was owned by the Cowell family. In the 1870s the Smoke House became a pub which went under the names of the Jolly Maltmakers and the Maltmaker's Arms. There was another malthouse just north of that.

## Francis Road

Francis Road was developed in the 1840s by John Francis, who lived in the White Horse public house at the corner with Crib Street. He built five parallel maltings running south off Francis Road which were known as the 'White Horse Maltings'. They were of brick with timber ends and identified as Nos. 26, 27, 28, 29 and 25. Nos. 28 and 29 had double kilns and a capacity of 32 qrs. – the others were single kilns and 16 qrs. John Francis was the first operator; later his widow lived in Alpha Cottage which is still there at the end of Francis Road. The maltings were owned until 1963 by Henry Page & Co. The Monks Row houses are now on the site. On the north side were The Omega maltings which ran through to Princes Street, then known as Omega Place.

## High Street

Jerome Murphy quoted a leaflet from Henry Page & Co. stating that "all the buildings between the south side of the High Street and the River Lea were once malthouses." A slight exaggeration but nearly the truth. It is borne out by the 1880 Ordnance Survey map (above). Maltings were established in this part of the town because leading maltsters had their offices and originally their homes in the High Street. The lists of maltsters in the early 19th century trade directories gives Water Row (the south side of the High Street) as the address of most of them. Maltsters needed to have a central office for dealing with other maltsters, farmers and representatives of the London breweries – the former inns in Water Row were ideal locations. An office on the main street was often backed by a 'home malting yard' behind the house. Here the pattern set by the former inns – an inn, a stable yard and then a garden, ending with a summer house or gazebo overlooking the river – was followed by the maltsters. Few if any of the malthouses established here reached as far as the river and there were no wharves here for loading malt on to barges.

*Maltings on both sides of the yard – and a stable with a horse –
behind Nos. 37 and 39 High Street. The main malting buildings survive
although the kilns have been demolished. The yard is now used by a
variety of businesses including the landlords, BaileyGomm Ltd.*

The old Saracen's Head Inn opposite New Road had its own
malthouse and there were maltings on both sides. Farther to the
west was a malting yard behind Nos 37 and 39 (see above).

Next door, long maltings ran back from the Ware Library of
printers Jennings and Bewley at Nos. 43-45 High Street and the
neighbouring garage of Gideon Talbot at No. 47. But both
properties along with their maltings were demolished in the
1960s as part of the Central Area Redevelopment and replaced
by modern buildings (now Peacocks and Greggs). The new
houses running down to the river behind Peacocks are known as
Swan Mews.

Next door at Nos 49-51 High Street was the Falcon Works –
Kiln Wire Manufacturer and Brass Founder. This business was
established by Charles Wells, whose tie plates are found on the
sides of many malt kilns in the town. The business passed to
Messrs A.J. Goodfellow & Co in 1859 and they carried on
working for the malting industry. A feature article in *The Pictorial
Record* of 1899 said that their wire floors for malt kilns and

*The Falcoln Works at 49-51 High Street*

their malting cowls were used in almost every malt producing county in Britain, and also for export abroad. Canon Travel and the printers Hertfordshire Display plc now occupy the premises.

Nos. 53-55 High Street was the seventeenth-century Raven Inn – a fine 'inglenook' fireplace exists inside Dandelyons and there is a good inn door in the wagonway next to Santander Bank. The maltings behind are now residential and known as 'Water Row' which was originally the name of the whole south side of the High Street.

At 57 High Street is the Saffron Building Society, which was formerly the Bull Inn with extensive maltings stretching back to the river. A plaque on the maltings show that the Bull itself closed in 1848 and the High Street building was refurbished as Ware Post Office in 1953. According to deeds owned by the late David Tappenden, this malting was owned successively by John Hillyard

1664, Aaron Cass 1710, Samuel Adams 1850 and Thomas B. Adams 1851. The maltings have now been developed for residential use as the 'Malthouse Mews'.

Behind Nos. 61-63 High Street (Aves and the 'Doctors' House') was an important malting site (illustrated above). Developed for malting in the late 17th century by the Docwra family – dated brick 1689 with M.D. (Mary Docrwa) next to the two-storey gazebo. George Docwra sold the site to Nathaniel Page in 1848; in 1874 it was owned by Mrs Ann Hudson who in 1877 sold it to her son-in-law, the maltster Henry Ward. In 1885, Henry Ward & Sons rebuilt the kiln and put the directors' initials in the brickwork. The yard then became the Home Yard of Henry Ward & Co. Malting here ceased in the 1960s. In 1965, the buildings and yard were sold by Henry Ward & Sons (Holdings) Ltd to Ernest George Smith, the business partner of David Tappenden. Together they founded the electronics company still located there, now known as Mode Lighting.

The Library Carpark was another 'home yard' – that of Henry Page & Co. Ltd. The yard was behind No 87 High Street, an 18th century house probably purpose-built for a wealthy maltster on the site of the Crown Inn; later it was owned by Edward Chuck. From Chuck the property and the yard passed to Henry Page, whose company, Henry Page & Co., bought the adjoining property, No 85, from Dr. William McNab – photographed above – and adapted it as the company's offices and later a laboratory where Jerome Murphy worked as head chemist. The only part of the malting to survive is known now as The Old Fire Station.

## Hoe Lane

The one malthouse in Hoe Lane is a nineteenth-century building, with a large brick kiln, constructed after the end of the Malt Tax in 1880, and a clap-boarded barley store at the other end with a lucam. The site is much older. It was owned in 1839 by John Cass and in 1863 by George Cass – the Cass family were an important malting family whose memorials are in the north aisle of St. Mary's church and who lived in Presdales House higher up Hoe Lane. The malting was later sold to Henry Ward & Sons who probably built the brick kiln. It was known as malting no. 20 and ceased malting in 1953. The complex probably originally incorporated the Royal Oak pub (formerly known as the King's Head and earlier as the New Haven brewhouse). The complex is now known as 'The Maltings' and used as a health and fitness centre and offices for Optrak vehicle routing software.

There was another malting in London Road behind the veterinary surgery, where a house called the Grange stood until 1972. It had a double kiln and a capacity of 32 qrs. and was owned by Henry Page & Co. The site is now occupied by Grange Gardens.

*The front and rear of Nos. 20-22 New Road, a timber-framed building and probably the remnant of an early malting*

## New Road

New Road has the oldest surviving malthouse in Ware – or at least part of one. Nos. 20 and 22 New Road is a timber-framed building of the 16th or early 17th century, which can be seen to be part of a malthouse because of the steep roof and small windows. It is the only survivor of the malting yard of the Dickinson family who lived in East Street. In 1690 the Christ's Hospital school complained that cinders from Mr. Dickinson's maltings were blowing in through the windows of Place House and they asked for shutters. The malting yard was closed and New Road built over it when the male line of the Dickinson family died out in 1829. That must have been when the malting at Nos. 20-22 was cut back.

Also in New Road are three parallel maltings (known as Nos. 1, 2 and 3), built in the 1830s for the production of 'brown malt' used in the brewing of 'porter beer'. At that time – with the coming of the railways – the Hertfordshire malting industry was in fierce competition with the maltsters of Newark, who supplied malt to the brewers of Burton-on-Trent. These brick maltings therefore incorporated a great deal of up-to-date Victorian technology. The kilns had wire floors, held in place by iron bars

*The three New Road maltings in relation to Christ Church – Bluecoat Yard is in the foreground.An aerial photograph of 1929 by Aerofilms from* www.britainfromabove.org.uk *© Historic England.*

which were fixed on the outside by tie plates – the tie plates bearing the name Charles Wells are still visible (Charles Wells ran the Falcon Ironworks in Ware High Street and specialised in fittings for the malting industry). The swivelling cowls above the kilns were also a Charles Wells invention – before his time, cowls were of the fixed 'mortarboard' design. The two northerly maltings are in private ownership and the Northern Malting has been developed for housing.

The Southern Malting, which is accessible from the Kibes Lane carpark, has been declared 'a community asset' and incorporates the Ware Arts Centre. It still has three malt floors in place, with a barley store and steeping chamber at the west end and the kilns at the east end. The wire floor of the kiln can be seen from the ground floor and the inside of the cowls from the first floor. The Southern Malting is the last surviving historic malting in Ware with its kilns in place and is listed Grade II by English Heritage.

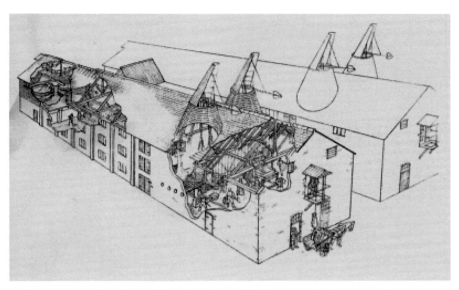

*A cut-away drawing of the Southern Malting, made by Andy Gammon in 2005, when the Ware Arts Centre was being refurbished. Architectural reconstruction illustration: © Andy Gammon Art & Design, Lewes - email: andyg.gammon@gmail.com*

*Below: the kiln of the Southern Malting, showing the tie plates that connected to rods holding the wire floor of the kiln in place.*

*Malting No. 50 in operation in the 1950s and
below while being demolished in the 1960s –
a photograph taken from the garden of No. 40 New Road and given to
Ware Urban District Council as a record.*

Farther up New Road was a large malting complex (known as No. 50), with an entrance to its yard next to No. 36 New Road where a garage has now been erected. It was built in 1879-85 by H. & A.D. Taylor of Sawbridgeworth (whose founder had been a malt factor in Ware). It was later acquired by Henry Page & Co. which sold it in 1942 to J. Harrington & Co. of Hertford. Malting ceased production here in the late 1950s and the buildings demolished in the early 1960s. Kiln House Close was then built on the site with access from Musley Lane to the north.

*The grandiose Park Road malting built by Caleb Hitch the Younger,
using his patent bricks and also more conventional bricks.
Behind the three-storey kiln are the malting floors.*

## Park Road

There was one malthouse in Park Road, a most impressive one
that still exists.  It consists of a three-storey malt kiln with the
later addition to the rear of two-storey malting floors in nine
bays.  It was built by Caleb Hitch II, using his patent bricks (also
found in the Rose and Crown pub in Watton Road) as well as
conventional yellow stock bricks and with lintels and string
courses in red bricks.  It was one of the first malthouses to have
an engine room, for an oil or steam engine to load barley on to
the malting floors.  It was operated by the Hitch family and later
by John Harrington & Son of Hertford.  It ceased to be used for
malting in 1964.

It was refurbished as an office complex and warehousing
for the new Asda supermarket, which opened in May 2015.

## Priory Street

There were two malthouses in Priory Street. The archway beside No 1 Priory Street gave access to a long building with two malting floors. Parts of this still exist as 'Abbot's House' behind a clap-boarded wall, but the main building was demolished and rebuilt as Yorke's Mews. The name came from Ray Yorke who moved his foundry and metal works from outside St. Mary's Church when that part of the High Street was opened up by Ware UDC for the Queen's Coronation in 1953. Farther along Priory Street, next to No. 44, is a former malting complex now known as 'The Malt House'. It is used for storage by Veolia, Interserve and other contractors for GlaxoSmithKline.

## Star Street

Star Street was the main wharfing area of Ware from which barges were loaded with malt and other produce for London. Consequently a large number of malthouses were established here. The 1851 Ordnance Survey Map shows as many as twenty malthouses and malt kilns.

Proceeding from the High Street down Star Lane (as it was then called) beside the Barge Inn, there were malthouses on both sides of the narrow street. The Common Wharf on the right had four malthouses with entrances on to it. One of these was later replaced by a corn drier owned by Henry Page & Co., which partially burned down in 1947, leaving two storeys which are now the Deans furniture store and Ware Bathroom Centre.

Farther along the south side of the street was one continuous line of malthouses, most of them with wharfs, broken only by the house which is now the Victoria pub. Even the 17th century 'corn stores' – a quadrangle of timber-framed buildings illustrated in Edith Hunt's *History of Ware* and demolished in the 1970s – was marked on the 1851 map as malthouses. Next to that were two maltings with a yard between. One of them was four floors high with Victorian double malt kiln and had the date 1900 set in the floor; the other was older with a tiled round malting cowl.

*Two views of the corn drier, built during the Second World War.*
*It partially burned down in 1947, leaving two floors.*

The last malting owner was Gripper and Wightman of Hertford and after 1954 they were used for storage by Thorn Electrical Industries. How the residential development acquired the name 'Omega Maltings' is a mystery, since that name properly belonged to a malting in Princes Street off Crib Street.

On the left-hand side, there were four malthouses, the first of which later became a milk delivery depot for the Cooperative Stores and has since been refurbished as a Sainsbury's store. Then there was a row of cottages before more maltings. There was no turning into Bowling Lane – that was only created in the 1930s. Then came the Ware Gas Works and after that open fields. But the Ordnance Survey map of 1880 shows three large parallel maltings occupying this field.

At the time of the malt tax – before 1880 – the malthouses on the north side of Star Street were Nos 8, 10 and 21; those on the south side were Nos 51 and 52.

All the Star Street maltings ceased operations in the 1960s. In the seventies those on the north side of the street were replaced by warehouses, which in turn were demolished and replaced by Star Holme Court. Bowsher Court at the corner of Bowling Road was built on the site of the Ware Gas Works.

*Cycling to work in Star Street in the 1950s.*
*The kiln fires were usually lit at 5 a.m.*

*Two views of the 'Omega Maltings' in Star Street.*
*Above: the older western range being used for storge in the 1960s –*
*the white hoist or 'lucam' on the right has been retained.*
*Below: the eastern range was rebuilt in brick after 1880*
*with a four-storey double kiln. A view from the river.*

## Watton Road

The two maltings on the corner of Park Road, which now form the Buryfields Maltings residential complex, were among the last to be used for making malt. They were of different ages. The more northerly one, partly of timber construction with a double brick kiln, is the older one and has the traditional revolving cowls. The Star Brewery was built at the malt store end of this malthouse, with the date C.H. 1862 for Caleb Hitch III (son of the patent brickmaker). The other malthouse to the south is also Victorian but was completely rebuilt in 1931 with an imposing four-storey kiln and fitted with the latest technology, including a Suxé coal-fired kiln with an electrical fan and mechanical turning of the malting barley. This was identified as Malting No. 23 with a capacity of 50 qrs.; the northern malting was No. 18 and had 40 qrs. capacity. They were owned by Henry Ward & Co. until 1963, then by Harrington Page & Co.

A malting occupied land behind the public house, formerly the New Rose and Crown, then the Worpell and now known as The Maltings. It was a brick building of five bays with windows.

*Two views of the Buryfield Maltings.*
*Above, in use for malt-making in the 1960s, looking towards*
*the Buryfield Recreation Ground.*
*Below, a view in the other direction after conversion to residential use.*
*Note that one of the lucam hoists has been retained and the other removed*
*to make way for a two-storey brick extension.*

# Sources and for further reading

Jonathan Brown, *Steeped in Tradition, The malting industry in England since the railway age* (University of Reading, 1983)

Aline Burgess, *The History of a Ware Family: Part I: Chuck and Collins* (Ware Museum, 1994)

Aline Burgess, *The History of a Ware Family: Part II: Page, Croft and Collins* (Ware Museum, 1994)

Christine Clark, *The British Malting Industry since 1830* (The Hambledon Press, 1998)

Maurice Edwards & David Perman, *Ware's Past in Pictures* (Rockingham Press, 1995)

Hertfordshire Archives and Local Studies (HALS) –
Henry Page & Co. D/EPa B6-B31
Henry Ward & Sons  D/EWd B1-B20
Trade Directories 1823-1929

Peter Mathias, *The Brewing Industry in England 1700-1830* (Cambridge University Press, 1959)

Jack Parker, *Nothing for Nothing for Nobody: a history of Hertfordshire banks and banking* (Hertfordshire Publications, 1987)

Suffolk Record Office, Ipswich –
Harrington Page Ltd. HC461/9